Contents

Cover: A Chinese poster shows workers
and members of the armed services fêting
Mao as the new leader of China
Front endpaper: Plaintiff and defendant abase
themselves in a magistrate's court, 1875
Rear endpaper: The last recruits
of the Kuomintang in Peking (photo by
Henri Cartier-Bresson)

Copyright © 1971: C P FitzGerald
First published 1971 by BPC Unit 75
St Giles House 49 Poland St London W1
in the British Commonwealth and
American Heritage Press
551 Fifth Avenue New York NY 10017
in the United States of America
Library of Congress Catalogue Card
Number: 70-134593
Made and printed in Great Britain by
Purnell & Sons Ltd Paulton Somerset

COMMUNISM TAKES CHINA

How the Revolution went Red

C P FitzGerald

American Heritage Press
General Editor: John Roberts

Introduction:
A China Transformed

The triumph of the Communist regime in China is the last, or as the Communists themselves would see it, the latest stage in the Chinese Revolution: a revolution which has taken place in one of the largest and most populous countries in the world, and is therefore a key event in the history of our age. Yet the country is far away, its character is known to most only by fictitious and contrasting caricatures, 'Willow Pattern Plate' landscapes with quaint figures, or 'teeming millions' toiling on barren farms. All caricatures have some element of reality, or they would have no meaning. Many parts of China have some of the most beautiful scenery to be found in the world; and in these idyllic surroundings there was both poverty and harsh toil. So huge a country is not uniform in climate or topography, but for simplicity can be divided into three major zones from north to south, each watered by a great river system. North China is the basin of the Yellow River and its surrounding mountain regions: cold and dry in winter, hot and for a short spell humid in summer, growing wheat and maize as its basic crops. This is the ancient 'China', the homeland of the civilisation, a great region of the temperate zone reaching northward to the borders of Siberia.

The central zone is the basin of the Yangtze River, the longest in the world. It has a hotter, wetter climate, with a short cool winter. The land is very fertile and rarely suffers from severe drought, which is the menace ever present in the drier north. In recent centuries, after full settlement, the Yangtze basin has been the most populous area of China, and the most advanced in all the pre-industrial arts and crafts. The southern zone, of which the chief centre is Canton, is the basin of the West River (Hsikiang): smaller than the other two, semi-tropical in climate, with only a short cool winter season. The Yangtze and the West River basins are the rice lands, and to northerners, collectively 'south China'. From the south also have come the migrants who now form the large over-

Left: A poster idealises the 1958 Great Leap Forward, Mao's over-ambitious campaign to industrialise China overnight

5

奋发图强 自力更生 建设祖国

走大寨之路

ZOU DA ZHAI ZHI LU

seas Chinese communities. These provinces speak a variety of dialects, whereas north China and the Yangtze speak 'Standard Speech', *P'u T'ung Hua,* formerly known to foreigners as 'Mandarin'.

There is another, historically very important division between the regions of China, not from north to south, but from east to west. West China is a mountain region, east China has the plains, the wide valleys of the lower reaches of the great rivers, and their rich deltas. Population is thickly concentrated on the plains and deltas, relatively sparse in the mountainous west. There are exceptions to this generalisation. In Ssuchuan, a great western province, there is a large, rich and very fertile plain; the south-east coastal provinces of Chekiang and Fukien are mountainous with only few fertile deltas and coastal strips. Shantung, a peninsula province in the north, is, in part, mountain country. This configuration means that all the great rivers flow eastward, rising far to the west in the Tibetan massif, and breaking out abruptly into the eastern plains from the high, steep escarpment of the western zone. They rise to flood levels in the summer when the eastern rains combine with the melting snows of the great ranges of the far west; in winter they are low. Summer is everywhere the wet season, under the influence of the south-eastern monsoon winds. Winter is dry —cold in the north, temperate in the south. This climatic situation means that in some parts of China almost any crop can be grown, and in some regions two crops can be raised on the same fields in one year.

China's industrial revolution

Until the most recent years, since the establishment of the People's Republic, the economy of most of the country was still in the pre-industrial stage, hand-worked agriculture and handicraft industry, including the celebrated silk spinning and ceramics. Modern heavy industry was rare and concentrated either in the port cities, where foreign concessions gave protection, or in Manchuria, which for long was under Japanese control. In the past twenty years this distorted pattern has changed; industry is now rapidly expanding in the north and north-west, where the main natural mineral resources are found. Cities which were little more advanced than in medieval times twenty years ago, such as Lanchou in Kansu province, are now great centres of modern heavy

Far left: The glorification of manual labour — posters urging workers at an oilfield to 'Rely on your own efforts and build up our motherland **(top)**, *and in praise of a village workforce* **(bottom)**. *Left: Traditional crowbar methods in use on an Indian border project. Iron discipline produced the new society*

7

industry. China has undergone an industrial revolution quite as important, and perhaps more profound in its ultimate consequences, than the political revolution which preceded it or the social transformation which accompanied it. In spite of this development the country is still basically agricultural. A vast population, estimated to exceed 600,000,000, must be fed. Weather vagaries from year to year threaten the harvest, and often cut it drastically. Land use and tenure must therefore be a prime factor in the Chinese economy for many years to come. Chinese industrial development is not aided from abroad by foreign programmes; what help was received from Russia was paid for, and the debt repaid in full. No further aid can be expected from that quarter. Foreign trade, although expanding, and purchases of foreign wheat, are marginal factors, even if the margin in food imports may be of crucial importance to certain areas.

Cracks in the old social system

Up to the land reforms inaugurated by the Communist regime, which culminated in the establishment of the commune system, land was held in China by private owners: either landlords renting their land to tenants, or peasants cultivating their own, usually very small, farms. The tendency since the last century of the Manchu Dynasty (19th) had been for landlord concentrations to grow and peasant proprietorship to shrink. This was a basic cause of social unrest and revolution. Landlords did not usually live on their estates, which were very rarely of great size but comprised the best land in the district. They resided in the cities, and bailiffs gathered their rents, using extortionate pressures to secure the maximum, from which they took their own ample share. This evil was historic, and the cause of many great peasant rebellions, often leading to a change of dynasty. Then there would be a new share-out of the land (theoretically all owned by the Emperor) and social peace would prevail for a time.

The social system was therefore unstable in the economic sense, but rigid in the class structure. Landownership went with scholarship, literacy, the monopoly of government posts and higher education. Tenancy or small ownership connoted illiteracy, poverty, often

Far left: Communism brought a fresh determination to strengthen China internationally. In 1950 Chinese troops invaded Tibet to assert a longstanding claim to suzerainty (top); the island of Quemoy, a refuge for Chiang Kai-shek's troops close to the mainland (bottom), provoked Communist shells in 1958. Left: 'Chinese Communist Forces aid Korea to slavery' — a UN leaflet (1952) protests at Chinese intervention in the Korean war

9

hunger, oppression, superstition, and latent rebellion. Great dynastic upheavals were followed by the deprivation of the losing side and the reward of the loyal victors, thus casting down some landowners and raising up some peasants, usually those who had taken up arms. The system, once more stabilised, continued with very little change. It became, in the 19th century, steadily less able to withstand the challenges of the modern world. Manufactures and the products of foreign industry undercut the native craftsmen, who were often peasants in origin supplementing the family income with their earnings. Unsuccessful foreign wars forced the imperial government into debt, and raised taxes which bore more heavily on a failing economy.

The ruling class, whether Manchu or Chinese, had been educated in the classics of Chinese literature, and discouraged from the study of such subjects as economics or even mathematics. These were left to merchants, a class without political power and much exposed to official pressures. The introduction of some modern industry and commercial methods in the Treaty Ports, where foreign powers held a privileged position protected by trade concessions, brought into existence a small new Chinese capitalist class, largely dependent on foreign connections and trade, very little in touch with the rural world of China, and hostile to, as well as jealous of, the power and authority of scholar landlord gentry. Shanghai, the modern city of hybrid architecture and centre of foreign economic power in China, was also the centre of Chinese capitalism and bourgeois nationalism. It was to become, before long, the centre of revolutionary conspiracy.

China under Communism

These features of the pre-revolutionary age have largely been transformed in the period of the People's Republic (the Communist regime). Land tenure by private owners has been eliminated. Landlord or small peasant proprietors' holdings were initially merged into equal, small farms, and later gathered together into co-operative farms in which former owners have a share no greater than that of former landless peasants; and finally the co-operative farms were grouped into communes which regulate the production and the labour distribution through subordinate 'brigades' and 'com-

*Far right: Solidarity against the imperialists. Dwarfing the figures of Churchill and Truman, Stalin and Mao stand pledged to 'Eternal Friendship' — in the event short-lived **(top)**; American imperialism is likened to a 'paper-tiger which frightens nobody' **(bottom). Right:** Watched over by Mao a lecturer educates the People's Liberation Army in the evils of capitalism*

panies'. All members of a commune are entitled to their share in its profits, its produce, and its facilities for education, health, and housing. The old pattern of rural China, both economic and social, has been wholly transformed. Private industry, never very widely spread, has been brought under public control, partly by the development of new state enterprises, and in much smaller part by the establishment of 'state-private' management, which permits the former owner to manage his enterprise for a fixed percentage of the profit, while the state controls marketing and supply. Even this residual aspect of capitalist control tends to disappear as the former owners die or retire and their sons do not wish to be associated with a 'bourgeois' way of life.

The elimination of landlord-tenant relations has also destroyed the social and economic base of the old ruling class. The educated, still probably predominantly of this origin, are now employed by the state in many capacities, technical, professional, scientific, academic and administrative. They have no connection with land or rent, and no monopoly of higher education or of government positions. Education has been enormously expanded, rather faster than the provision of jobs suitable for the newly-qualified to fill. This has caused some unrest and was a factor underlying the Cultural Revolution of 1966-8. The role of the former scholar gentry was, for the first eighteen years of the People's Republic, filled by the members of the Communist Party, themselves very largely of scholar gentry descent, but also including ex-soldiers and officers of the revolutionary war, peasants, and industrial workers. The Cultural Revolution upset the exclusive position of the Party, and has introduced new elements, the nature and future character of which are still obscure, but the presence and increased role of the Army is conspicuous. In the new society it is less easy to identify social class with economic base. The peasants of the communes are indeed still rooted in the soil; but industrial workers, an expanding class, are given functions which go well beyond the management of their own unions or even the enterprises in which they work. To be literate and educated is no longer the distinctive mark of a ruling class and, as the spread of primary education rapidly expands, illiteracy is no longer the mark of the poor.

China's place in the world

In another important respect post-revolutionary China differs profoundly from the society which it overthrew. From the beginning of the 19th century down to the consolidation of the Communist regime after 1950 China had been internationally a weak nation, militarily nearly impotent, and ineffective in the councils of the world. The

country was protected from foreign conquest and partition more by its size than by its might. It was easy to defeat Chinese forces; to pacify and govern so vast a region was a daunting prospect. Thus China was relatively strong in defence, if she was ready to sacrifice herself in a prolonged resistance. This was proved by the abortive Japanese invasion.

By 1970, China, having developed her economy to some degree on modern lines, has concurrently acquired military power, not on the scale of the USA or the USSR, but sufficient to make an attack upon China a most hazardous enterprise and to cause her neighbours, and even more distant countries, to fear her possible ambitions. China has also adopted an uncompromising attitude in foreign relations, partly in response to the policy of isolation (or 'containment') which foreign powers have endeavoured to sustain. These are dangerous attitudes on both sides, and may prove disastrous to the world. They are, nonetheless, direct consequences of the Chinese revolution in its political, economic and even social aspects. The revolution was primarily a response to internal pressures and problems which seemed to admit of no other solutions. But the consequences have overspilled to create a new international situation with which neither China nor her rivals have yet come to terms.

In pre-revolutionary times the Chinese had a markedly ethnocentric view of the world and their place in it, a view based on a long historical tradition of being the most civilised people within their range of knowledge. Today, partly under the inspiration of an internationally orientated doctrine, Communism, and perhaps more still in response to the new stimuli of technology, natural science and modern ways of living, the Chinese people are confronted with the need to reshape their world outlook and make a more realistic compromise between the pride of national power regained and the need to live in a world which must always be wider than their own. Foreign nations need to admit that China exists, that she cannot be controlled from outside, and that the Chinese people are not only the most numerous but one of the most gifted peoples of the earth. The Chinese were slow to adapt their ancient society to the modern world; they had the reputation of being the most obdurate conservatives, and nothing less probable than a Chinese revolution which would end in the creation of a new type of society, dynamic, restless, innovating, and iconoclastic would have been imagined in the 19th century.

Left: The vanguard of the Cultural Revolution: youthful Red Guards, launched by Mao to shake up an increasingly conservative officialdom, chant from the Red Book of Mao's Thoughts

13

Chapter 1
The Origin of the Chinese Revolution

In the final year of the 18th century the Emperor Ch'ien Lung died; he was well over eighty years of age, had reigned for sixty years, and abdicated four years before his death. He was the third of the great Manchu Emperors who had made their Ch'ing dynasty one of the most powerful in Chinese history, ruling an empire larger than ever before. China then appeared a great and powerful state with which no foreign power would dare to meddle. Forty years later the British invaded its coasts with ease and took some of its greatest cities: 100 years after the death of Ch'ien Lung the Manchu empire was at its last gasp. The Chinese revolution was to break out twelve years later, and 150 years after the death of Ch'ien Lung China was a Communist-governed republic.

The process of this transformation can be considered as really beginning with the death of the aged Emperor and the rapid decline of the power of his successors. Troubles within the empire were soon compounded by foreign assaults and defeats which, in turn, led to further economic crises and internal rebellions. The ancient system, which had lasted for more than 2,000 years, failed to meet the new problems and became a cause of their aggravation.

In one sense the Chinese, not many years after Ch'ien Lung's death, were ready for a change. The dynasty had fallen into decline, like many others before it; it would therefore fall, but this would not be a real revolution: another dynasty, probably a Chinese one, not an alien house like the Manchus, would replace it. There would be a great renovation in practice and authority, but the ancient system would go on. Several factors prevented this expected development. The long peace which early Manchu rule had imposed upon the empire had led to a great increase in population, and a shortage of land for cultivation. No new industrial development arose to alleviate this pressure. Chinese technology, a few centuries earlier in advance of the rest of the world, had

Left: Boxer propaganda print depicts the siege of the hated foreign settlements at Tientsin in the Boxer Rising of 1900

Ports
- Great Britain
- Russia
- Germany
- Portugal
- Treaty ports all European

Occupied territ
- Great B
- Russia
- France
- Germa
- Japan

Areas of influer
- Great B
- Russia
- France
- Germa
- Japan

RUSSIA

MONGOLIA

MANCHURIA

Tungchow
Peking
Port Arthur
Tientsin
Vladivostok
CHIHLI
KOREA
Yellow R.
TIBET
Sian
SHANTUNG
Weihaiwei
Tsingtao
Wuhu
Shanghai
Nanking
Ningpo
Chungking
Yangtze R.
INDIA
Amoy
BURMA
Canton
FORMOSA
LAOS
Hong Kong
Macao
Kwangchow
Kiungchow
SIAM
CAMBODIA

stagnated, in part because the government patronised Confucian classical learning and gave no countenance to science or technology, in part because the social system, which put power into the hands of a landed educated class, gave little scope for commercial enterprise and no political power to merchants. The educational system was opposed to innovation, the ruling class was the product of this education, and succeeded only by passing very stiff examinations in classical learning.

The second cause was the increasing contact with the outside world, represented by the maritime trading nations of Europe. Their trade had profound, but not always beneficial, effects on society. When the British found that opium commanded a ready market in China and helped to finance the British rule in India, the import of this drug rapidly attained huge proportions, doing great harm to the Chinese economy, to the revenue, and not least to the health and competence of the ever-expanding number of people who smoked it. The grandson of Ch'ien Lung, the Emperor Tao Kuang, attempted to suppress the traffic, which was nominally illegal. The measures he took led to a clash which developed, in 1840, into the Opium War. In two years China had been heavily defeated, mainly by the loss of important coastal cities, but including the fall of Nanking, the southern capital of the empire, 200 miles up the Yangtze. The Manchu dynasty had never favoured naval power which they feared would be a danger to them, as based on the southern disaffected provinces. The war was ended by the first 'Unequal Treaty' by which the British gained concessions at several ports, including Shanghai, the cession of the island of Hong Kong, and a privileged position for their traders and missionaries. Other powers soon claimed similar rights by virtue of the 'most favoured nation' clause in this Treaty of Nanking.

The T'ai P'ing rebellion
The dynasty had lost prestige, and the diversion of trade in silk and tea to Shanghai from Canton created great unemployment and distress in some of the southern provinces. These discontents led ten years later, in 1851, to the rebellion of the T'ai P'ing movement, a religious sect based on half-understood Christian teaching. This movement won immediate and sweeping success in the south, took Nanking in 1853, and there established 21 ▷

*Top left: European intervention in China and the Far East in the late 19th century. **Bottom:** The foreign 'barbarians' at the court of Peking—a caricature by Gillray in 1793 of Lord Macartney's embassy to the Emperor Ch'ien Lung. Otherwise indifferent to the west, the court welcomed its ingenious gifts*

The old order

The collapse of Imperial China in 1911 ended a period of traditional rule that had lasted for over 2,500 years. During this time the system of government and the class structure remained unquestioned. The imperial dynasty ruled by the Mandate of Heaven. Rebellion might succeed in changing the dynasty but fundamentally it altered nothing. Obedience to the system was encouraged by Confucian orthodoxy, which saw change as synonymous with decay. Perfection resided in the Golden Age of the remote past, innovation was a corrupt departure from the great original. The apparent immutability of Chinese society—typified by the street scene in Kiangsi **(left)**, with public letter-writer and barber installed, and by the three high-ranking civil-service mandarins **(below)**—deceived both foreign observers and Chinese scholars. The tempo of change was increasing under the impact of the modern world, and stability was soon to be shattered by real social and political revolution

a rival dynasty, the T'ai P'ing Heavenly Kingdom. For eleven years the Manchu dynasty had to struggle to survive this challenge, complicated by the revolt of Muslim communities in west China, and by a further war with Britain and France in 1856, ended in 1860 by the Allied capture of Peking itself. Yet four years later the Manchu dynasty was able to suppress the T'ai P'ing rebellion and gradually recover the territories lost to other rebels in the west. These events had greatly altered the situation in China. The dynasty had been saved not by its Manchu troops, but by Chinese armies raised and commanded by Chinese officials who now held great power. Only their loyalty to the throne kept the Manchu dynasty from collapse. The experience of a long war had taught the new commanders the value of many western weapons and inventions. They began a cautious movement of reform to re-equip the Chinese armies with modern weapons and provide steamships for transport.

Foreign pressures increase

The first stirring of reform was thus a direct consequence of foreign contact, and a response both to internal rebellion and foreign attacks. The empire had proved weak in its own defence, and the age of confident European imperialism was dawning. The treaty which ended the Second Opium War in 1860 inflicted heavy sanctions on China, opened new ports, and obtained new privileges for the foreign trader. The system, now fully operative, has been called semi-colonialism by modern Chinese writers. It meant, in practice, severe limitations on China's sovereignty. But the foreign powers who benefited from it accepted no responsibility for the government of China. It was not then realised that the consequences would be the decay of the Chinese state until a revolutionary solution became inevitable, and that such a revolution, when it came, would sweep away the foreigners and their privileges. Most foreign observers were, on the contrary, convinced that reform and modernisation in China would greatly improve their own situation and expand their trade.

Chinese control over its tributary kingdoms around the fringes of the empire was eroded and eliminated in the second half of the century. The French took control over all Vietnam after a short war with China in 1883-5. Russia had added large tracts to the Siberian and Central Asian territories in 1860 and in 1871, although these areas were remote and not inhabited by people of Chinese race. Britain annexed Burma in 1885, and the Japanese,

Left: In 1860 the Anglo-French attack on the Taku forts outside Tientsin cleared the way to Peking and fresh concessions

joining the new imperial race, defeated China in Korea in 1895, and annexed Korea outright in 1910. As a consequence of the Sino-Japanese War of 1894-5 the Russians obtained a dominant position in the Manchurian provinces and built a railway across the country to the warm water port of Lushun (Port Arthur). Early in the next century the Japanese fought the Russians in Manchuria — although Chinese territory — and took the southern half of the country under their dominance as a reward of victory (1905).

The autocracy of the Empress Dowager

The dynasty, since the death of the Emperor Hsien Feng, in 1862, had been without an adult monarch. Hsien Feng was succeeded by his only son, a child, under the regency of his mother the Empress Dowager Tz'u Hsi. He died of smallpox within two years of his majority. The Empress then put upon the throne another infant, who reigned as Kuang Hsu, although he was of the same generation as his cousin, the late Emperor, and therefore, by dynastic law, ineligible for the succession. Other possible candidates were too nearly adult for the Empress Dowager's ambitions. The second regency continued until 1898, when Kuang Hsu, briefly exercising some authority, conferred his favour on the reform party and, after the 'Hundred Days of Reform', was virtually deposed and actually confined for the rest of his life by a coup d'état organised by his aunt, the Empress Dowager Tz'u Hsi. She then continued to rule the country until her own death in 1908, on the day following that of Emperor Kuang Hsu. Before she died thus unexpectedly, she had placed on the throne another infant, the four-year-old P'u Yi, who was to be the last Emperor of China. This half-century of the rule of an autocratic and reactionary woman, largely ignorant of the modern world, was the main reason why no modernisation of the monarchy on Japanese lines could be effected, and a prime cause of the reform movement turning to revolutionary policies.

Kuang Hsu, although educated in the strictest antique manner, ignorant of modern matters and of any foreign language, was by nature of an enquiring mind and free from the vices of his predecessors. He earnestly sought to recover the power of the state and the prestige of the dynasty. Reformers such as K'ang Yu-wei obtained his confidence and inaugurated a headlong, rather uncoordinated programme of reforms, known as the 'Hundred Days of Reform'. These measures taken as a whole were inadequate, but were intended only as a first step. All of them, considered wildly radical at the time, were to be

Left: The Japanese landing at Port Arthur in the war of 1894

23

accepted without question a few years later. The Empress Dowager abolished them all, when she took power once more, with the exception of the creation of the modern imperial university at Peking. This institution, the Peking National University of later times, became the intellectual seeding bed of the whole modernisation movement, and a most powerful instrument of cultural change within China. Had the Empress Dowager understood how to arrest the reform movement, this was the institution which, above all other reforms, she should have destroyed. It is perhaps a measure both of her ignorance and of the growing strength of the new forces in society that she did not do so.

Dr Sun Yat-sen and the republican movement

After the imprisonment of Kuang Hsu and the flight or execution of his followers there was no further hope for a reformed monarchy which could have led the country to a peaceful solution of its problems. The reformed monarchist movement withered away from lack of any visible leader on the throne. K'ang Yu-wei, the reformist leader, still holding the same views as he had in 1898, lived on for many years to become an anachronism, the last monarchist. Young China, as it was now beginning to be called, the generation which grew to manhood at the turn of the century, turned to revolution and the republican doctrines of Dr Sun Yat-sen. The leader of the revolutionary movement was not of scholar gentry origin, but the son of a poor farming family near Canton. At an early age he migrated to Hawaii, where he obtained his schooling. Having graduated in medicine at the Hong Kong Medical College (forerunner of the university) he practised for a time, but soon turned to revolutionary politics. Dr Sun was of mainly foreign education, never very expert in the written Chinese language, and as much at home in foreign countries as in China. He accepted the radical ideas of the period, as preached in Europe and the USA: the idea of republic, because monarchy was both out of fashion and, in China, represented by an alien dynasty, a point felt more strongly by southerners than by men of the north; the idea of democracy, because parliamentary democracy was the model he observed in all advanced Western countries. Neither his writings nor his ideas, however, reflected the realities of the Chinese social world.

For several years he pursued his aim of overthrowing the dynasty with tireless zeal, but scant success, and inadequate planning. It was not until after the end of the century that he gained widespread support among the Chinese students studying in Japan, who were for the most part from well-to-do and educated families. He also found support and derived funds from the overseas Chin-

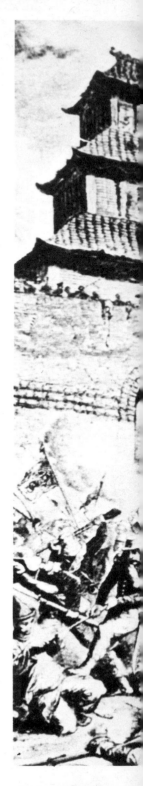

ese communities in South-East Asia and the USA who suffered the disabilities which the low status of China in international affairs imposed upon them. Nationalist enthusiasm was often strongest in these expatriate groups. Dr Sun's early revolutionary efforts were directed towards seizing the city of Canton, a centre of disaffection from the dynasty.

Canton was certainly anti-Manchu, but it was not China, nor typical of China. The revolutionary movement remained weak until it began to gain support in the more central parts of the country, above all in Hunan, an inland southern province, and in the great international port of Shanghai. When the revolution broke out it did not begin at Canton, but at Wuhan, the river port city of central China, and it was initially the work of the army, not of civilian conspirators. At that date Dr Sun Yat-sen was fund-collecting in the United States.

The Boxer Rebellion

In 1900, ten years before the fall of the dynasty, the movement of violent xenophobia, known as the 'Boxer Rebellion', had swept north and north-west China, causing a further loss of prestige and sovereignty to the declining dynasty. Originally anti-dynastic, and sparked by the misery due to drought and flood in the province of Shantung, the 'Boxers' — their real name was the 'Society of the Harmonious Fist' — turned against the privileged foreign missionaries in their midst. Such peasant uprisings have been frequent in Chinese history, and usually inspired by mystical and magical beliefs, such as the invulnerability of adepts of the faith. The anti-foreign direction of the movement became quickly associated with support for the reactionary party now dominant at Court, and thus was soon being used by the dynasty as a last source of identification with the people, even although this meant conniving at violent and murderous attacks upon foreign residents in China. After the Boxer armies had been allowed to enter Peking, where they committed many outrages on all suspected of foreign sympathies or even foreign ways of life and dress, there followed the assassination in the streets of the capital of two foreign envoys, the German Minister and the Counsellor of the Japanese Legation. Thereafter, the Boxers, **28** ▷

*Left: Savage hand-to-hand fighting in the Boxer revolt: from a contemporary illustration. **Next page:** A French cartoon vilifies the avenging European relief force **(top left)**; portrait of the Empress Dowager Tz'u Hsi, a bastion of reaction whose abortive attempt to use the uprising for her own dynastic purposes heralded the end of the monarchy **(bottom left)**; nemesis for the Boxers—their headless torsos await crating **(right)***

supported by Muslim troops also in the capital, besieged and attacked the foreign legations.

The Court wavered, promising protection to the foreign residents, but allowing the Boxers to wreak their fury. The Empress Dowager seems to have been deliberately deceived by some of the Manchu princes, who were out-and-out reactionaries, into thinking that the foreign powers intended to restore the Emperor Kuang Hsu, and impose a virtual protectorate on China.

The strange siege, in which the Chinese refrained from using the heavy artillery which would have destroyed the legations in a day or two, dragged on for several weeks. The first international relief force of sailors and marines, hastily landed from warships, was not strong enough to reach Peking. A second, much more formidable army commanded by a German Field Marshal was now landed at Tientsin, after the foreign forces had destroyed the Taku forts which guard the approach to that port. This action was taken as a declaration of war by the Court, which now found itself at war with all the major European powers, and America and Japan as well. Peking was taken on 14th August 1900 and the Court fled to the west of China. Subsequent negotiations imposed new and severe limitations on China's sovereignty, and led directly to the virtual occupation of all Manchuria by Russia. The southern viceroys would take no part in the Boxer War and concluded *ad hoc* agreements to maintain neutrality and order in their provinces with the foreign consuls in Shanghai. Thus the latent division between north and south, present since the suppression of the T'ai P'ing Rebellion, was made more emphatic.

The other main result of the abortive attempt to expel all foreign influence and remove all foreign residents — an objective wholly out of line with reality in the world of that time — was to turn the whole nation towards revolution. The dynasty, having at foreign insistence executed or exiled all the princes of the reactionary party — except the Empress Dowager herself — tried, in these last years, to implement a policy of reform which far exceeded anything proposed by the unfortunate Emperor Kuang Hsu. It failed to win support, and when, in 1908, the Empress Dowager died the day after the imprisoned Emperor, the last regency in the name of the infant Emperor Hsuan T'ung (named P'u Yi) was wholly ineffective, ridden with faction, and incompetent. The mood of the country was radical; no one really supported the outworn monarchy; even its own members were without confidence and initiative. The failure of the Boxer Rebel-

Right: 'China in distress', helplessly present at her own carve-up at the hands of the imperialists. A French cartoon of 1898

28

lion destroyed any remaining chance of averting revolution. It was only a question of time and opportunity.

The end of the Manchu dynasty

The actual outbreak, on 10th October 1911, was accidental. An explosion in a house used by republican conspirators for the making of grenades alerted the police, who discovered a list of names of republican party members. These included those of many officers of the garrison. Realising that only quick action could save them, these officers forced their commanding officer, who had had no part in the conspiracy, to choose between proclaiming the Republic, or death. General Li Yüan-hung chose rebellion. At once a large part of southern China overthrew the dynasty. In many places no resistance was offered, the army joined the revolution, many imperial officers and officials did the same; within a month only the northern provinces remained under imperial authority, and in some places this was already very uncertain.

The Court was forced to call upon Yüan Shih-k'ai, the general who had backed the Empress Dowager in her dethronement (or rather confinement) of the Emperor Kuang Hsu, and had been dismissed by that monarch's brother, the actual Regent. Yüan insisted on full authority, both military and political. With this granted he made a brief campaign at Wuhan by which he demonstrated that the northern army was both loyal to himself and stronger than the revolutionary forces. Then he began to bargain with the republican side to dethrone the dynasty, peacefully, and ensure for himself the chief position in the republic. This deal was consummated early in 1912. The Manchu Dynasty abdicated, set up the Republic by imperial decree as its successor, and was granted what would have been very favourable terms, had they ever been carried out in full. Yüan Shih-k'ai was made provisional President, and Sun Yat-sen, who had first assumed that office, withdrew. The nature of the revolution of 1911-12 was thus peculiar, and had long-lasting and unfortunate consequences.

The failure of the revolution of 1911 to solve China's problems, which indeed it tended to aggravate, has obscured certain aspects of the developments of that time which can now be seen as of long-term significance. Contemporaries, both in China and abroad, saw nothing but the collapse of a decadent order and the blunders and follies of its incompetent or presumptuous successors. Yet the decision to replace the dynasty, and the monarchy, with a republic was, at that time, a most radical step. In 1911 there was no republic in all Asia, and only two, France and Switzerland, in Europe. The political form which was viable in the United States did not ap-

pear to be particularly commendable in South America. That the Chinese, of all people, should choose a republic rather than a new dynasty seemed to be wildly idealistic, unpractical, and reckless. Later developments in China may have cast some doubt on the view that the Chinese are an inherently conservative people; what was not understood at the time was that, after 100 years of the deplorable failure of conservative policies and attitudes to safeguard the nation or advance its interests, the Chinese were in the mood for a radical change both of form and concept. To the astonishment of many Western observers there was no such phenomenon as a monarchist party seeking a restoration. Yüan Shih-k'ai's attempt to enthrone himself proved to be unacceptable even to men as reactionary in other matters as he was himself. The Manchus themselves hardly indulged in the pipe dream of restoration. If the Chinese are by nature sometimes conservative, they are also extremely realist.

'Young China' begins to stir
The pace of social change in society as a whole matched the radical departure in political forms. Both dress and hair style altered: the queue was cut off, the gorgeous robes of imperial office went to the curio shops. Literature was soon to experience the profound transformation of the substitution of current colloquial speech for the classical style, which cannot be spoken and had remained unchanged for upwards of 2,000 years. Before long, mass education, using a limited range of ideographs, was to make popular education on a large scale possible for the first time in Chinese history, thereby laying an essential foundation for all further political and economic advance. Higher education, rapidly expanding with the foundation of many new universities, attracted the best of the scholar talent to itself, enlisting men of the old 'book perfumed' families, who no longer found any opening for a career in the corrupt and chaotic political life of the shaky republic. The new learning, both Western and scientific, on the one side, and a fresh and unprejudiced approach to Chinese history and literature on the other, opened a whole world of intellectual endeavour to the younger generation. They were intensely idealistic, patriotic, and inexperienced; they were also disgusted with their government, ashamed of the debased standing of their country, and determined to regain 'Wealth and Power', the national goals which one of the first of modern Chinese Western-educated intellectuals, Yen Fu, had set before his countrymen. All this ferment in society and among the educated class was largely ig-

Left: *The revolutionary army puts an end to the pigtail, 1911*

31

nored, or disdained, by foreign observers. They spoke and wrote with studied contempt of 'Young China' as foolish boys intoxicated with half-comprehended notions derived at second-hand from missionary teachers. Few foreign residents in China, including the resident correspondents of the national newspapers, could read Chinese. The scholars who could were interested in the literature and history of the past, and rather disgusted by the innovations of the young modern Chinese. The intellectual aspect of the revolution of 1911-12 was almost entirely unobserved by the Western world, which concentrated its attention on the political confusion and economic decline. This failure to understand the real forces and recognise the true sources of change was to mislead Western opinion and policy for the next thirty years. Among the phenomena of that age least understood in the contemporary Western world (if now rather more familiar to those countries) were student unrest, demonstrations, and political agitation on a mass scale. These were some of the first significant products of the revolution of 1911 and its aftermath.

Yüan threatens the republic

Meanwhile the first years of the new republic had proved a political disaster. The Provisional President, former imperial commander-in-chief Yüan Shih-k'ai, from the first showed that he was out to build himself the position of a dictator independent of Parliament, and soon began to plan the overthrow of the republic and his own accession to the throne as first Emperor of a new dynasty. Having obtained a very large loan from foreign bankers which made him independent of Parliament, he dissolved it when he had coerced it into electing him as full President. When republican opposition was aroused in the south by these acts, he easily crushed it with armed force. Dr Sun Yat-sen fled into exile once more; other prominent republican leaders were removed from office, and the most able leader of the Parliamentary Republican Party, Sung Chiao-jen, had already been assassinated at Shanghai, on the orders of Yüan. The great powers seemed to accept the new President as their best hope of keeping order in the country; the Parliament had proved incompetent, corrupt, and self-seeking. Almost its only valid act was to vote its members large salaries; votes were offered and sold on the stock exchange. Early in 1915, with the Western powers at war with each other, Yüan began to prepare for his usurpation of the throne.

The plan seemed to go well; a subservient consultative assembly recommended the restoration of the monarchy;

Right: Dr Sun Yat-sen presides over a cabinet meeting, 1913

Yüan was invited to ascend the throne; he declined thrice, in the best classical tradition, and then accepted. It was announced that the new dynasty would be inaugurated at New Year in 1916. Disenchanted with the republic, the nation seemed ready to accept the new monarchy, if not with enthusiasm, then with acquiescence. It was true that Yüan's prestige had been damaged by the Japanese presentation of the Twenty-One Demands, which if accepted in entirety would have made China a Japanese protectorate in all but name. The Japanese did not love Yüan, an old opponent in Korea in former years. The Emperor-elect had managed to reject the most obnoxious of the Demands, but had to accept others, and the transaction was highly repugnant to patriotic young Chinese. But the republican movement was fragmented and suppressed; the reaction to Yüan's monarchical scheme came from his own generals, suborned, as it has been said, by Japanese money. On Christmas Day 1915 one of them, in the far south-west province of Yunnan, raised a revolt in favour of the republic. Yüan at first thought it a trifling affair, but the troops he sent to suppress it went over to the rebels, or retreated without engaging them. More and more defections occurred, until the movement became a landslide. Early in 1916 Yüan, at the insistence of generals still nominally loyal, had to 'postpone' the new dynasty and then, postponement failing to meet the demands made upon him, to renounce the throne on condition that he remained President for life. It is uncertain whether this would have been accepted either; but in June 1916 Yüan died. His health had been poor, but the Chinese people considered that he had died of 'eating bitterness' — of frustrated ambition.

The generals who had contrived his downfall installed one of their number as President, but he was powerless. From the death of Yüan the country rapidly dissolved into a number of virtually independent provinces, ruled by despotic viceroys, warring upon each other, all hoping to control Peking and its revenues, all seeking to oust the one who had for the moment gained the prize. The Warlord Era had begun.

Right: The transformation of the Chinese army as depicted in a French magazine. On the right are Chinese soldiers of 1911

Chapter 2
The Early Republic: The Warlord Period

The death, in June 1916, of the frustrated would-be Emperor, Yüan Shih-k'ai, inaugurated the most depressing period of the Chinese revolution, usually known as the Warlord Era. It lasted for just over ten years, and the memory of this period of confusion, weakness, social deterioration, and international impotence, has bitten deep into the consciousness of the modern Chinese. It has also left an unfortunate and durable impression upon the minds of foreign observers and commentators on Chinese affairs. The belief that the union of the Chinese nation is fortuitous, or temporary, or the product of unusual circumstances, and that the natural destiny of the country is to be divided and weak, still lingers, and is at once revived the moment some new internal political contest gives any apparent confirmation. Much comment on the recent Cultural Revolution reveals this continuing misapprehension. Wider and more extensive knowledge of Chinese history shows that the warlord period was what Chinese historians have long ago designated as an 'Age of Confusion'—a period, shorter or longer, following the fall of one great dynasty and the rise of a successor. In some respects the warlord period conforms very well to this established pattern. It was brief, it was most certainly confused, and the unity of the country was virtually destroyed. Also, it was followed by the rise of the new and durable regime.

In the period 1916 to 1928 no claimant sought—openly at least—to found a new dynasty, nor even to restore the monarchy in any form. All merely sought power and money under a nominal republic which was the internationally recognised Chinese state. The mark of the warlords was their total lack of any ideology and their personal greed. Money was more important even than power, for power was brief, and served only to offer the best chance for enrichment. Once wealthy, the military leader would allow a rival to supplant him, and retire, with his booty, to the safety of the foreign concessions in Shanghai or Tientsin, where his wealth could be safely

Left: The leader of a warlord firing squad signals success

37

placed in foreign banks immune from Chinese jurisdiction.

The age of semi-colonialism

It was thus the new factor of foreign power that perverted and distorted the ancient contests of an Age of Confusion. The fact that this same foreign domination placed the collection of the Chinese Customs and the Salt Monopoly (known as the Salt Gabelle) under foreign control, in order to safeguard this revenue and secure the loans which foreign investors continued to make to powerless and venal governments, is the main justification for the term 'semi-colonialism' with which the modern Chinese describe the plight of their country at this time. It was also the only reason for preserving the fiction of a central government and a cohesive state. The foreign customs collectors worked for the nominal Peking government, collecting revenue in ports under the military jurisdiction of the warlords, but remitting revenue to Peking. Once the service of the foreign loans, the first priority, had been met, the Peking government was in theory free to dispose of the surplus, which was still large. This was the prize for which the warlords contended: whoever controlled Peking could lay hands on this revenue, and no rival who did not control Peking had any part of it.

After the death of Yüan, Dr Sun Yat-sen had rallied the republican faithful, including the rump of the short-lived Parliament, at Canton, where, with the dubious support of local warlords, he set up a government which claimed to be the legitimate one, but was denied recognition by the foreign powers. It was also denied the customs revenues collected in Canton itself. Short of funds and lacking any trained military support upon which he could rely, Dr Sun's regime was overthrown in 1918 and the republican leader withdrew to the French Concession in Shanghai.

Warlords rampant

Meanwhile, in the north, there had been a sudden brief attempt to restore the Manchu dynasty, engineered by a very reactionary and brutal commander, Chang Hsun. Suddenly occupying Peking, he proclaimed the young ex-Emperor P'u Yi once more, and for ten days the dynasty 'reigned' again, although only in Peking. The northern warlords, outraged at this attempt to forestall what many of them secretly aspired to perform, united to overthrow Chang Hsun. Peking was retaken with some token fighting; P'u Yi retired to the seclusion of the Forbidden City, being officially exonerated from complicity in the 'Restoration'. The leading militarist reshaped the Peking regime, and before long accepted the

pressure put upon him by the Entente Allies to declare war on Germany. The main object was to seize the German shipping laid up in neutral China's ports.

The move was very unpopular with the educated classes of China. From this time the country was in effect divided into several virtually independent states; Chang Tso-lin, a former bandit turned general, controlled Manchuria, under the aegis and toleration of the Japanese, who dominated the economy of those provinces. The warlord in control of Peking exercised his usually short authority in the metropolitan province of Hopei and adjacent Honan. Shanghai and the adjacent region was the domain of another warlord. The middle Yangtze was ruled by local men of less power, and the western provinces had each its warlord, the unfortunate, large but rich province of Ssuchuan having to support the burden of no less than three, who continually warred upon each other. Taxes in 1923 had been collected — in advance — up to the fifty-sixth year of the republic, that is, 1968.

China 'betrayed' at Versailles

The south was under its own leaders, men who nominally claimed to be supporters of the 'legitimate' republic in Canton, but who in practice ruled their provinces just as independently as those in the north and centre, except, if possible, worse. Such was the condition of China as the First World War came to an end, and the republic of China, as one of the victor powers, sent her delegation to the Versailles Peace Conference. Her delegation was led by and composed of experienced diplomats, men of education and culture, who had for the most part served abroad for many years. The diplomatic service of China was the last refuge of the old gentry within the governing establishment. They had the unenviable task of representing a country which all the world knew to be chaotic and powerless, and endeavouring in these discouraging circumstances to uphold its rights and claims.

They were soon to learn how hard this task was to be. China claimed the return of the leased territories in Shantung province which Germany had forced her to yield in the late period of the Empire. A Japanese and a small British force had taken the port of Tsingtao from Germany in 1914, since when Japan had administered the occupied territory. It was now discovered that by a secret treaty the Allies had promised Japan the reversion of these German interests in order to enlist her support in the war. China was to get nothing back. She was offered the termination of German extra-territorial rights

Left: The 'Age of Confusion' — scenes like this were frequent in a period when rival warlords contended for power and easy profits

and the return of the few and small German concession areas in Tientsin and Hankow. It was believed in Allied circles that this could do no harm to their own interests, and would put German business at a great disadvantage in the post-war period.

The 4th May uprising

The consequences of this betrayal, as the educated Chinese saw it, were momentous, and have been recognised by later observers as a landmark in the development of the Chinese revolution. When the news was made public, in May 1919, a sudden and spontaneous movement of protest arose among the university students, mainly at the National University of Peking, which soon won much wider support. There were massive demonstrations in Peking, culminating on 4th May 1919 — a date which has given its name to the movement — in the burning of the houses of the corrupt ministers who had, as was said, 'sold the country to Japan' and the destruction of their motor cars on the streets, a technique of demonstration familiar today, but then new. The police, who were called upon to fire upon the student demonstrators, did so with some reluctance, and few fatalities. The agitation did not cease, and the more disreputable politicians were forced out of office. The other main achievement of the demonstrations was that the Chinese delegation at Versailles refused to sign the Treaty, and China has never been a signatory to the Peace of Versailles. This action at least preserved China's legal claim to the Shantung leased territories, although Japan remained in *de facto* possession.

The 4th May movement had other less conspicuous results. It roused the educated class in China, particularly the younger generation, to a full realisation of the state of their country both internally and in the world at large. Nationalism, as opposed to republican idealism, was born. The new enthusiasts did not much care what form of government was adopted so long as it did something to restore China. Belief in the parliamentary form of democracy waned; it had not worked, and it was seen as associated with the very Western countries who had preferred Japanese power to Chinese rights.

The Russian Revolution at this moment offered an alternative which, to very many educated Chinese, at once appeared preferable. Many young Chinese became ardent nationalist patriots, but had no understanding of or liking for Communism; others were attracted intellectually to the doctrines of Marx and Lenin, which

Left: *The 4th May uprising in Peking: outraged students protest against the humiliating conditions of the Treaty of Versailles*

now began to appear in translation, and almost all were deeply impressed by the transformation of Russia from an outworn absolute monarchy to a socialist republic. They saw that the intervention of foreign powers had failed to arrest the Russian Revolution. Russia was feared as well as hated by the Western capitalists. This offered to weak, chaotic China an instructive example. China, too, had overthrown her outworn imperial system; but with what result? Chaos, corruption, weakness and decline. The view that this deplorable consequence of the idealistic revolution of 1911 was due to taking the wrong policies and ignoring social problems became common among intellectuals. Marxist literature and left-wing ideas took root in China long before a Communist Party had been formed. These ideas and views continued to influence the younger generation, whether Communist or Nationalist. In this sense the Communist Party of today is certainly right in commemorating 4th May 1919 as a crucial date in the history of the rise of Communism in China.

Outwardly, 4th May made little difference to the warlords who still ruled in China. They could discard unpopular ministers, their puppets for the day, without trouble. They could still pursue their feuds and struggles for wealth and power without heeding student unrest. From 1920 their civil wars became an almost annual event, timed for the long dry autumn, when the harvests had been gathered. The term of power of any one clique was now a bare year; in the provinces some warlords had more stable positions, and their contests were for more marginal prizes than the rich revenues nominally controlled by Peking. The pattern of civil wars, destructive to the peasant population, but light in casualties among the mercenary and unmotivated soldiery, seemed unbreakable. Banditry flourished, nourished by the numerous deserters from defeated armies. The rich landlords fled the disorder to the strong cities, leaving bailiffs to collect what rents they could. These agents found that only by enlisting military support and sharing the revenues could they collect any rents at all. The difference was placed upon the peasant tenants. Thus warlord rule contributed massively and directly to the ruin of the peasantry, the collapse of the economy, and social disorder.

The semi-colonialist foreign powers appeared indifferent to this situation, and blind to their own responsibility for much of it. Order was maintained in the Treaty Ports, where their investments were placed and their business carried on. It did not seem to occur to anyone that this mixture of privilege and irresponsibility

Right: *Dr Sun Yat-sen's troops search a village for bandits*

could end in an explosive situation. Few foreigners could read Chinese, and those few were more interested in the Chinese classics than the literature of their own time. The movement of opinion to the Left was largely unknown and unsuspected by the foreign resident in China, or his government at home. It was regarded as irresponsible 'Young China' agitation by the few who perceived it.

Birth of the Kuomintang

Dr Sun Yat-sen was living in Shanghai. There, in January 1923 he had an interview with a Soviet envoy, Adolf Joffe, from which arose an agreement by which Dr Sun obtained Russian support to restore his authority in Canton, which local warlords had usurped. Dr Sun had hoped for British or American support for this purpose, but had been denied. He had, from the first, admired the Russian Revolution and, like most Chinese of his time, saw nothing horrifying about the methods used to carry it out. 'Woe to the conquered' was always the fact of Chinese political life; that fallen monarchs should lose their lives did not surprise or particularly shock them.

The Sun-Joffe conversations were of great importance, for already there existed the newly-founded Chinese Communist Party, and these talks helped to regulate the relations which were to determine the roles of the two parties during the coming crucial years of the revolution. It was agreed that the Soviet system was not suitable for China, whose principal need was to achieve unity and free herself from the restrictions imposed by the Unequal Treaties. On the other hand the new Nationalist Party was reorganised, and, now known as the Kuomintang, was ready to welcome individual Communists as members, and these members would not be required to leave their Party. It was an ambivalent relationship, which produced some unexpected results.

The Soviet Union had already won the approval and support of wide classes of educated Chinese by its unilateral renunciation, as early as the summer of 1918, of the special rights and privileges, extraterritorial jurisdiction over Russian subjects, concessions and leases, which the Tsarist government had enjoyed along with other Western nations and Japan. This renunciation, treating China, for all her confusion, as an equal and not as a 'semi-colony', was in sharp contrast to the retention of similar rights and concessions by all the Western powers. The USSR sent its first envoys to Peking in 1922, but diplomatic relations were not formally resumed with that nominal government until 1924, when the Russian envoy, Karakhan, styled Ambassador (while all other

Right: *Swift justice — a street execution in the Warlord Era*

44

powers had only a Minister), became automatically the head of the diplomatic corps, to the great mortification of his Western colleagues. But while these formal gestures were made to Peking the real Sino-Russian contact of significance was with the Canton regime, and with Chinese student Marxists.

The founding of the Chinese Communist Party

In 1920 the Russians sent George Voitinsky and a Dutch Communist named Maring to China to organise a Chinese Communist Party. It was founded, formally, in July 1921 at a secret meeting in the French Concession at Shanghai. Twelve delegates from cells in different parts of the country attended. The delegate from Hunan was Mao Tse-tung, who had founded the Hunan cell. Two well-known Marxist professors of Peking National University, Li Ta-chao and Ch'en Tu-hsiu, were also founder members, although neither of them could attend this first meeting. Ch'en became the first Secretary-General of the Party. There were only fifty or so members at this time, but when the Party held its third meeting in June 1923 the membership had risen to 432.

The Party had by that time already a record of having organised and promoted more than a hundred strikes in Shanghai and other southern cities, including the successful Chinese Seamen's strike, which won considerable (and overdue) concessions for the seamen. Its prestige rose rapidly, and this fact induced Dr Sun to agree to Communists joining his own Kuomintang as individuals. The Communist Party at first reluctantly, but under pressure from the Comintern (Communist International), ratified this decision at its third meeting in June 1923 at Canton.

At this time Dr Sun Yat-sen was able to return to Canton and, with the aid of his new Russian advisers, organise his own army and free himself from the domination of local self-seeking warlords. Thus the revolution had now a secure base from which both Parties, in alliance, could operate. Dr Sun appointed a man of thirty-six, who had had some experience as a revolutionary officer in 1911 and 1913, but had subsequently gone on to the Shanghai Stock Exchange, as the organiser of the new army, and sent him to Russia for a course in more up-to-date military tactics. This man was Chiang Kai-shek. Thus both Mao and Chiang came into some prominence, if only in revolutionary circles, at almost the same time. Their careers were to run on until the present day in contrast and in conflict.

Left: In Canton Dr Sun Yat-sen (on left) strengthened his base with the aid of the Russians Blücher (centre) and Mamaev

47

Northern militarists did not seem to appreciate the threat to themselves very clearly, although they took up strong anti-Communist attitudes, asserting that the whole revolutionary movement was Communist. This it was not, but the presence of Communist members and Russian advisers certainly gave colour to the accusation. It was generally accepted by foreign observers; even years later Chiang Kai-shek was still 'a Red' to many of them. The Chinese Communist Party was, in fact, an infant in the leading strings of the Comintern; Maring took part in its inner councils, and Russian direction was still paramount.

In the Kuomintang there existed other groups, with whom Chiang Kai-shek was to become associated, who took a cooler view of the Russian involvement. The Western Powers had refused to aid Dr Sun, preferring the doubtful durability of various northern warlords, who in fact drove each other out of Peking every second year. The dominant motive of Western policy was still the search for the 'strong man' who would 'put China's house in order' and, by doing so, safeguard the investments, the trade and the privileges of the foreign businessman. Whether such a dictator would do anything to satisfy the aspirations of the Chinese people, or raise the condition of the peasantry, does not seem to have been taken into account.

A turn of the wheel in the late autumn of 1924 had driven the warlord favoured by the British, Wu P'ei-fu, from Peking and given power to his former subordinate, Feng Yu'hsiang, known to the foreign residents of China as the 'Christian General'. Feng indeed professed Protestant Christianity, and was wont to baptise his troops, *en masse*, with a garden hose: but he was also inclined to the revolutionary cause; he renamed his army 'Kuominchun' (the People's Army), which had obvious links with the name of the Nationalist Party – Kuomintang. He also abruptly broke the agreement for Favourable Treatment which had been concluded between the republic and the ex-dynasty, and bundled the shadow Emperor P'u Yi and his court out of the Forbidden City into exile at a few hours' notice. This showed republican fervour, and before long Dr Sun Yat-sen had decided that Feng Yu'hsiang was a genuine revolutionary who could at last provide him with the support he needed to transfer his government in one bound to Peking, confront the Powers with a *fait accompli*, and force them to recognise the Kuomintang as the true legitimate government of China. He left Canton and journeyed – by sea – to Tientsin and then to Peking to negotiate this happy conclusion of the

Right: *Sun Yat-sen's death briefly united the nation in mourning*

civil wars with Feng Yu'hsiang. Unfortunately matters were not so simple.

The death of Sun Yat-sen

Dr Sun was himself a sick man, and as it soon proved, fatally ill. Feng Yu'hsiang had not the power he supposed himself to hold, and was soon menaced by formidable rivals. Other northern warlords did not relish the prospect of the end of their era of power, and the creation of a new revolutionary government backed by one of their number who had hitherto held only a subordinate position. When Feng Yu'hsiang turned upon his commander, Wu P'ei-fu, in October 1924, the latter was engaged in a large-scale attack upon his chief rival, Chang Tso-lin of Manchuria. Feng's rebellion ended this, but made Chang the ally of the rebel Feng. Wu retired to the Yangtze valley. Chang Tso-lin claimed his share of the spoils in the traditional manner; the new government in Peking had to have a large component of Chang's men, and other warlords claimed their part. Feng was by no means the master of north China. Thus Dr Sun found a disillusioning situation in the capital. He became very ill, and died in March 1925. With his death, courteously celebrated by all factions as that of a national hero with magnificent pomps, all hope of a quick solution vanished. Before long Feng was ousted from Peking, and Chang Tso-lin ruled in his stead. It was in this disappointing hour that fortune gave Nationalists and Communists alike a chance to recoup their losses.

No peace for the foreigners

On 30th May 1925 students demonstrating in the Nanking Road, the principal shopping artery of the International Settlement in Shanghai, on behalf of strikers who worked for a Japanese textile mill, refused to disperse when one of their number was arrested by the settlement police. They assailed the police station to which he had been taken; the police ordered them to disperse, they did not do so, and the police, commanded by a British officer, opened fire. Eleven students were killed. The effect of this incident was prodigious: in comparison the 4th May 1919 riots in Peking were a tea party.

A violent wave of xenophobia swept China from north to south. A total boycott of British and Japanese goods was proclaimed and enforced by a spontaneously organised force of boycott pickets, which soon came under strong Communist influence. A second tragic shooting

Left: Chiang Kai-shek (right) with the Panchen Lama. China in 1925 was too divided to reassert her authority over Tibet

51

incident in Canton, where a procession of demonstrators was fired upon by persons still unidentified, but immediately assumed to be Concession police, led to the mass withdrawal of Chinese labour from Hong Kong, paralysing the trade and life of that colony. Missionaries in the interior were forced to withdraw in haste to the coastal cities, foreign travellers, if British, were exposed to popular wrath, and only Germans wearing armbands marked 'German' in Chinese could safely walk the streets of Canton. Alarmed and amazed at this reaction to what they thought was a legitimate, if perhaps over-severe, police response to a riot, the foreign powers were soon induced to send troops and ships to Shanghai to safeguard their nationals, the authorities of the International Settlement declaring that their volunteer forces and police could not guarantee law and order. Bewildered and assailed with a violent propaganda offensively phrased the foreign community in China hardly understood what had happened, or why.

To Chinese, Chinese of every party and persuasion, it was crystal clear: in Shanghai, a Chinese city, Chinese citizens, and students at that, had been shot down by foreign-employed police, for demonstrating against the exploitation of their fellow countrymen by foreign capitalists. It was a gross violation of China's sovereignty, of humanity, of justice and of political power. No one in authority could stand up to this strong emotion; the Peking government, dependent on a warlord who was himself a client of the Japanese, wavered, made feeble protests, which the powers rebutted, but did not dare to act against the boycott and demonstrations. In southern cities, and in Canton, the capital of Dr Sun's Nationalist regime, the authorities were even less able to control the situation, and often did not in practice do anything against the boycott. In Canton it was actively supported by the regime in power. Nationalism received an immense, nation-wide impulse: peasants and workmen who had a few weeks before not known one kind of foreigner from another now talked of British and Japanese with hatred, and of others with more toleration. Such phrases as 'running dog of the imperialists' and 'thieves who sell the country' were commonly used — and printed — referring to the government and its officers and ministers. The army, or warlord armies, which did not dare to make war upon the foreigner, were derided as useless ciphers.

All this was a vast help to the revolutionary forces, both Nationalist and Communist. They had been given that national issue, simple, clear, and easily understood,

Right: *A portrait of Sun Yat-sen and the flags of the Kuomintang greet the anniversary of the abolition of the monarchy*

which was what they needed to rouse the mass of the people. The foreigner was to blame for all China's ills, aided by the vile compliance of venal politicians and mercenary warlords. To the Nationalists, it was the foreigner who played the devil's role; they were not so keen to incriminate the Chinese ruling class and its wealthy backers. The Communists treated the foreigner and his aggressions and pretensions as the direct consequence of a weak, corrupt and socially unjust society. To them the foreign evil would be cured by, and only by, a social revolution which would destroy the old society and build a better one. Then the foreigner would quickly be shown to the door. In this division there were already apparent the seeds of the future split between the two parties, but in 1925 and 1926 the unity and drive were still dominant.

The collapse of the warlords

Even before 1925, the Canton regime had been building up its strength to contest for power with the warlords who controlled the rest of China. Now they actively pushed forward these plans, encouraged by the obvious demoralisation of their opponents and their supporters. The risk that such a new civil war, if victorious, would bring the revolution into open conflict with the Western powers, and with Japan, was not one which dismayed the Communists. They expected such a conflict, and would have welcomed it as forcing all patriots on to their side. The Nationalists, as was to be soon apparent, were not so sure that war with the Western powers would promote their interests. In the white-hot fever of national resentment and anger, which the Nanking Road shooting had sparked off, these differences were obscured, and certainly not apparent to the foreign observers and their governments. When, in 1926, the Nationalist Northern Expedition started from Canton and invaded Hunan province as a first step, foreign opinion rallied to the warlords, to anyone who would oppose the 'Red revolution' which they saw approaching. The warlords were broken reeds; Hunan quickly capitulated, the revolutionary armies advanced on Hankow, which with its sister cities Wuch'ang on the south bank of the Yangtze, and Hanyang on the opposite bank of the great tributary river the Han, together form the urban complex now called Wuhan, one of the largest centres in China. It was defended by Wu P'ei-fu, but not for long. His troops put up slight resistance. By late autumn 1926, Wuhan had fallen to the revolution.

After Wuhan had fallen the revolutionary government was transferred to that city and operations to advance down the Yangtze to Nanking and Shanghai began. They were hardly opposed; the armies of the war-

lords melted away, their men had no stomach for a fight against fellow-countrymen with whom they often sympathised. All south China went over to the revolution, and the western warlords, remote from the scene of action, but equally remote from Peking, found it wiser to make gestures of goodwill or of nominal obedience to the new regime. Winter held up the advance for a while, but early in 1927 it resumed.

The Nanking outrage

Chiang Kai-shek, who commanded the whole army, approached Nanking; but he had spent the winter at Nanchang, capital of Kiangsi, and his attempt to have this city made the new capital had been rebuffed by the Party leaders, who had proclaimed Wuhan as capital on the 1st January. Chiang was now close to a breach with the left wing of the Party, and had conferred at Nanchang with wealthy supporters and their emissaries from Shanghai. On 22nd March, after a previous failure, the Communist-organised Shanghai Workers' Union and other left-wing bodies including many of the former boycott pickets, carried out a successful coup in the Chinese-ruled part of Shanghai and ousted the local warlord's troops. Two days later the Nationalist army captured Nanking, but at the moment of their entry some of the troops committed outrages on the foreign residents, killing several. Foreign gunboats bombarded the city to cover the evacuation of the survivors. This incident brought the Western powers and the revolutionary armies to the brink of war.

It has always been alleged by Kuomintang apologists that the killings at Nanking were carried out by units under Communist officers. This was not the belief of some British consular officials who were in the city at the time; they are firmly of the opinion, supported by good evidence, that the units concerned were in no way to be distinguished from any others in the army. In truth after the bitter feelings of the previous year it was hardly surprising that indoctrinated troops, whether led by Communists or Nationalist officers, should get out of hand in the moment of victory, which, they had been taught to think, was as much over the foreigner as over their warlord-led countrymen. But when Chiang arrived in newly-liberated Shanghai — the Chinese-ruled part of that great city — he found a tense situation. The foreign powers were almost ready to drive him out, as the commander responsible for the Nanking slaughter; the foreign residents regarded him as a dangerous 'Red'. Suspicion and ill-will ruled between his officers and the Communist-led urban insurgents who now held Chinese Shanghai. Chiang was also

Left: Workers on the move — a revolutionary militia, 1925

at odds with the government in Wuhan which had moved to the left.

On 3rd January 1927, only three days after the inauguration of the Wuhan government, a crowd of workers organised by the Communist Party and led by Liu Shao-ch'i, who was to become later one of the chief leaders of the Party and the principal victim of the Cultural Revolution, invaded the British Concession at Hankow, which adjoined the Chinese city along the waterfront. The police were overwhelmed, there were no adequate naval forces to be landed, and the Concession was taken over by force. Earlier in the summer of 1926, the British had stationed a cruiser at Hankow to guard against such an eventuality. But in winter the Yangtze level falls low; although a large ship can remain at Wuhan through the low water months, it cannot be taken downstream across the rapids which appear in winter. To avoid the risk of having a cruiser immobilised for months at Wuhan, the British Naval authorities withdrew the ship when the river began to fall. The British government realised that the Hankow Concession could not be regained without a major naval and military operation, 400 miles inland, and then only when the spring arrived. Shanghai, near the sea, could be defended at all seasons. It was decided to let Hankow go, and with it the much smaller Concession at Kiukiang, a river port half-way downstream to Nanking. An officer of the British Legation in Peking, Mr O'Malley (later Sir Charles), was sent to Hankow to negotiate an agreement for the retrocession of the two Concessions.

The Wuhan government thus had scored a major diplomatic victory over the 'imperialists', while the armies of the commander-in-chief, Chiang Kai-shek, had won no such renown in a similar encounter. This was a further aggravation of the differences which now marred Chiang's relations with his civilian colleagues at Wuhan. When they proposed a new structure of command, which would have reduced him to only one among a number of equal commanders in the field, he recognised that the parting of the ways had come.

The rift widens

On the 12th April 1927, a day infamous to the Communist Chinese, Chiang carried out a sudden bloody coup against the left-wing forces which controlled Chinese Shanghai. Thousands were slain, and hundreds executed without trial. The atrocities perpetrated have long been

Left: The foreigner became the scapegoat for China's ills.
Top: A picket boat patrols the Pearl River, Canton, during anti-British riots in 1925. **Bottom:** British troops on guard near the entrance to the European quarter of Shanghai, 1927

remembered, and form that 'blood debt' which the Communists claimed in their hour of victory twenty-two years later. One of the few Communist leaders in Shanghai to escape, and that only by quick wits and luck, was Chou En-lai. A similar coup, two days later, put Chiang in full control of Canton; on 24th April he proclaimed a new Nationalist government seated at Nanking. Wuhan repudiated him, and retained the support of the Communist Party, but it was the weaker of the two governments in military terms.

The Wuhan government only endured another three months; it was headed by Wang Ch'ing-wei, an old revolutionary from imperial times, who was generally regarded as the real successor of Dr Sun Yat-sen, although as a civilian he never commanded the military support which brought Chiang Kai-shek to the leadership. Although Wang was then counted among the left-wing Nationalists, he and his colleagues increasingly distrusted the Russian adviser, Borodin, and the Communist members of the government. Nationalist military officers came from the rural landlord class; they were disturbed to learn that the rural revolutionary organiser, Mao Tse-tung, was active in Hunan preparing a social revolution which would most certainly be directed against the landlords. Moscow was still urging the Communist Party to keep in alliance with the Kuomintang, but the Kuomintang of all factions was increasingly averse to this policy. The Indian Communist, Roy, is said to have precipitated the crisis by indiscreetly showing Wang Ch'ing-wei a telegram from Moscow which indicated that the Communists should remain with the Kuomintang in order to control it from within.

Wang and the Nationalists then decided to break with the Communist Party. On 15th July 1927 the Communist Party was expelled from the government, its militia in Wuhan disarmed, and the Party declared an illegal organisation. Borodin, Roy, and some of the leading Chinese Communists, including Madame Sun Yat-sen, the widowed second wife of the old leader, left for Moscow.

The Communist Party reacted at a secret meeting early in August by deposing its first Secretary-General, Ch'en Tu-hsiu, who had advocated the Comintern line of continued alliance with the Kuomintang, and by giving full support to the revolutionary line which Mao Tse-tung, among others, was advocating.

On 31st July at Nanchang, Chiang's former headquarters in Kiangsi province, the local forces under Communist officers seized the city. They failed to win over the larger Nationalist formations in the vicinity, and on 5th

Left: French tanks protecting the Shanghai concessions, 1927

59

August were driven out and retreated southwards into the mountainous interior of the province. This mutiny was led by Chu Teh, who was to become the legendary and famous leader of the Communist armed forces; one of his subordinate young officers was Lin Piao, who is now the designated successor to Mao Tse-tung. At the time the incident was hardly noticed; but it was the foundation date of the Red Army which was to fight through many vicissitudes to ultimate victory twenty-two years later.

The next month, September 1927, the Wuhan government dissolved and amalgamated with the new government at Nanking, from which Chiang Kai-shek had tactfully withdrawn, nominally to promote unity, in fact to avoid open conflict with Wang Ch'ing-wei, while keeping undercover control of his military support. He went to Japan, where he married the daughter of a Christian Chinese pastor in Shanghai, Soong Mei-ling, one of three sisters, the eldest having married H.H.Kung, a banker and descendant of Confucius, the second being the widowed second wife of Dr Sun Yat-sen. Thus the 'Soong' dynasty, as they were to be called, came into the forefront of Chinese politics. The brother, T.V.Soong, an old friend of Chiang's since his stockbroking days, became the financial wizard of the new regime.

Chiang returned to power in the early days of 1928, having created in Nanking a political climate which made his rival Wang Ch'ing-wei unable to retain power. At the end of 1927 the revolutionary movement was finally split between the two parties, Nationalist and Communist. The former was far the larger in membership, had control of the government, and was soon in the next year to overthrow the last of the warlords, Chang Tso-lin of Manchuria, and bring the government in Peking to an end. For the next ten years the government presided over by Chiang Kai-shek at Nanking became the legitimate government of China, recognised by all the powers. It maintained a ceaseless and ever more powerful assault on the Communists in insurrection in the southern mountain provinces, yet, far from being crushed, the Communist Party was in reality gaining strength.

Left: *Mao mobilises the new-style people's army. His revolutionary line was accepted by the Communist Party in August 1927*

Chapter 3
Nationalists and Communists

To observers in China at the time, and to most Chinese also, the events of 1927 appeared decisive: the revolution had passed under the control of moderates, even of right-wing elements. The Communists had been disowned and crushed. There might be mopping-up and pacification measures needed in the interior, but the ultimate complete triumph of the consolidated Kuomintang appeared certain. Nothing in the history of the Communist Party at this time seemed to contradict this assessment. After the failure at Nanchang the Red Army withdrew southward through Kiangsi, entered Kuangtung province and, in late September 1927, attacked and occupied the important port city of Swatow. This success was brief; within a few days it was driven out, and retreated to pass the winter in a relatively inaccessible coastal area of Kuangtung. In the same month Mao Tse-tung, who had been charged with the task of raising a Communist revolt in his native province of Hunan, failed completely before Ch'angsha, the capital, and only narrowly escaped capture and execution. It is said that he was in fact made prisoner, but not recognised, and escaped his captors who thought he was an ordinary peasant. From this debacle he fled with a handful of followers to the mountain stronghold of Chingkangshan, on the border of Hunan and Kiangsi. This had always been a lair of bandits, conveniently located on the border so that if one provincial government attacked it, the other was sure not to co-operate. In December the southern Red army had attacked Canton itself, aided by an internal rising organised by the Russian Communist, Neumann. The city was held for two days, but then recaptured with great slaughter by the Kuomintang general Li Ch'i-shen. Many years later, rallied to the side of the People's Republic, Li Ch'i-shen ended his days as a Vice-President of the Republic; but the monument at Canton which commemorates the thousands he executed in 1927 still records those facts. There are aspects of Chinese political life which do not conform closely to European models, east or west.

Left: Nationalists clumsily prepare to hunt Mao's guerrillas

Defeated in the south, virtually a fugitive group, Chu Teh and the remnants of his force made their way north into Hunan and, early in 1928, joined Mao Tse-tung on Chingkangshan. This event has been hailed in Communist history as a great turning point in their fortunes, and the meeting on Chingkangshan is a favourite subject of current art. It was indeed significant. In their remote retreat Chu and Mao formed that partnership which was, years later, to bring victory to their cause; they reorganised their forces, enlisted men, enforced the distribution of landlord property among the poor peasants. A systematic policy of indoctrination and military training began to build up that hard core of guerrilla fighters, dedicated to their cause, which was to be the instrument of the long resistance to superior Kuomintang numbers, and the key to final victory.

The irrelevance of Moscow

Compared to the new efficiency and order which Chu and Mao were creating in the wilds of south China, the central organs of the Communist Party, now withdrawn to the comparative safety and secrecy of the French and International Settlements at Shanghai, presented a deplorable spectacle of intrigue, misapprehension, and doctrinaire pedantry. The Politburo was dominated by the Moscow-trained men who took orders from the Comintern and never dared to question them. After the failure of the military campaign in south China, for which he was held responsible, the Party's sixth congress, held in Moscow, deposed Ch'ü Ch'iu-pai from the Secretary-Generalship, and put in his place another urban-orientated man, Li Li-san. Li had devoted all his work to promoting and leading strikes. He believed that only in the great cities, backed by proletarian workers, could the revolution succeed. Activities among the rural peasantry of remote provinces were creditable, but essentially marginal. The Russians believed that the world-wide recession of 1929-30 would create a revolutionary situation in all industrialised countries, and that the Chinese movement must be prepared to seize upon such a development. Concentration on urban revolution was thus all important.

In fact this consideration was largely irrelevant to China: only the ports where foreign business was important were seriously affected by the Great Depression. Rural China continued to live its own detached life, and suffer its own, rather different evils. A weak and often divided leadership in the clandestine party organs at Shanghai was unable to comprehend the realities of the countryside, and had at this time very little influence on

Left: Chinese 'big sword' troops train for the Japanese threat

what Chu and Mao were doing. What influence they had was unfortunate.

In 1930, still endeavouring to follow Moscow's instructions, Li Li-san ordered Chu Teh to attack Ch'angsha, capital of Hunan, so that at least one large city should be available as a focus for real Communist revolution as he saw it. Chu managed to seize the city, but was too weak to hold it for more than ten days. He succeeded in withdrawing to the mountains without severe loss.

Displeased with Li Li-san, as with Ch'ü Ch'iu-pai before him, Moscow decreed that Li must be deposed and sent to Russia for retraining. He went, and did not return to China till 1949. Authority under the direction of Russian advisers was now entrusted to a group of 'returned students' — young men who had been educated and trained in Moscow. They were no doubt well instructed in Marxism, but they were very ignorant of China.

It is surely true that, but for the guerrilla movement inaugurated by Chu and Mao, the Communist movement would at this time have lost all momentum and probably have diminished to an ineffectual intellectual protest with minimum support. Few people, except the vigilant Nationalist police and their ardent allies, the foreign police of the concessions, were really aware of the existence of the clandestine Communist Party, and fewer still counted it as a factor in Chinese politics. On the other hand, the whole nation was soon to realise that the guerrillas represented a real force, which the government found troublesome and was failing to destroy. After the first reorganisation at Chingkangshan, Chu and Mao were able to work with very little opposition for nearly three years, and this respite was to prove of great importance to their future survival.

Chiang Kai-shek and the Extermination Campaigns
Chiang Kai-shek had larger fish to fry: in spite of the apparent triumph of his wing of the Kuomintang, he was opposed and confronted by a number of dissident military rulers who had not fully abandoned the warlord outlook, or who were jealous of Chiang's authority. The Kuangsi group, among the most competent of the Nationalist generals, resisted his authority in the south; and in the north he had, in 1930, to meet a full-scale rebellion led by political opponents such as Wang Ch'ing-wei and backed by military figures such as Feng Yu'hsiang. It took nearly a year to overthrow this movement, more by corrupting its lesser military supporters than by prowess in the field.

Left: A prisoner captured by the Japanese in Manchuria wears the belt of machine-gun bullets with which he is to be shot. By the spring of 1933 Japan had occupied the whole of Manchuria

In the end it was the co-operation of Chang Hsueh-liang, the son of Chang Tso-lin and still warlord of Manchuria, which turned the scale. Chang, in turn, was a possible rival when he had ousted the rebels from Peking.

These preoccupations, which seemed so much more serious, had prevented Chiang from mounting any large-scale campaign to crush the Kiangsi-Hunan Communist insurrection. It was already growing formidable when, in late 1930, Chiang felt able to strike against it. The First Bandit Extermination Campaign, as he designated this operation, was launched in November. The strength of the Red Army was about 10,000 men, Chiang's forces much greater. But their invasion was met by the famous guerrilla tactic which Mao has immortalised: 'When the enemy attack, we retreat; when he halts, we harry him; when he retreats, we pursue.' The Nationalists withdrew foiled, and with heavy loss. The next year, 1931, undeterred, but also uninstructed by this experience, Chiang tried again, twice, in the Second and Third Extermination Campaigns. The Red Army had greatly increased in number, and was now estimated to be 300,000 strong. This was no mere gang of bandits; Chiang was faced with a major rebellion.

The second and third campaigns were no more successful than the first. The second became bogged down, and the third had to be called off when, in August 1931, the Japanese seized Manchuria and appeared to threaten a wider war against China. This was averted by China's virtual acceptance of the loss of the three provinces, some of the wealthiest in the country. It was not a situation which added to the prestige of the Nanking regime, and their concentration on fighting the internal foe rather than the external enemy began to excite criticism. The first movement of public opinion towards a more sympathetic approach to the Communists can be traced to the policy of 'internal pacification before resistance to external pressure' which Chiang affirmed.

There were other signs of public disillusionment. In February 1932 the Japanese had attacked Chinese forces in Shanghai from the eastern part of the International Settlement. A desperate and prolonged struggle took place, in which the local Chinese forces resisted with courage and success for several weeks. They had been supported by an immense volume of public opinion in Shanghai itself, and the aid of many voluntary organisations. But the Nanking government had given none and

Left: A wry German view of Japanese intentions: Japan occupies Manchuria (top left), defeats the Chinese (top right), is warned off by the League of Nations (bottom left) and deliberately mistakes the Note as a cue to devastate the region

had sought, throughout the conflict, to find a way of appeasing Japan and ending the struggle by a local settlement. This was done, and the defenders were transferred to the province of Fukien, where they could have no contact with Japanese.

Fukien adjoins Kiangsi; it could have been possible for the Chinese Communists to open lines of communication with the Nationalist army in Fukien, which was ill-content with its treatment by the Nanking government. That regime was now about to mount a still more massive onslaught on the Kiangsi Communists who, in November 1931, had set up a formal Communist republic in that province with the small city of Juichin as its capital. It was defended by at least 300,000 men, and controlled nearly 300 counties, not all of which were contiguous, and some were situated on the borders of other provinces. There were in all now eleven 'liberated areas' in southern and central China.

The June 1932 Fourth Bandit Extermination Campaign exemplified the new scale of the war. Chiang's forces numbered more than 500,000, the struggle lasted for nearly nine months, until March 1933, and ended in the clear defeat of the Nationalist army. Three divisions were wholly destroyed, two divisional generals taken prisoner, more than 10,000 rifles were captured. The Nationalist forces had to withdraw to base. The defeat of the Fourth Campaign was the high point of the Kiangsi Soviet Republic, which was soon to experience grave problems.

Mistakes of the Communist leadership

The clandestine Politburo in Shanghai now found that, in addition to the great risks of detection, arrest, and execution to which they were constantly exposed, they were also becoming remote from the scene of real Communist power — that they were in danger of losing control. It was decided to move to Juichin, the capital of the new republic.

This move was effected apparently without the knowledge or interference of the Nationalist security organisation, which thereby reveals itself as somewhat less than competent. But from the point of view of Mao Tse-tung and Chu Teh it might have been better if the Nationalists had been more vigilant.

The Returned Student Group, who still led the Party, now could exert direct influence upon policy in Kiangsi. According to Communist official history it was their mistakes which directly led to subsequent disasters. They are blamed for rejecting any accommodation or alliance with the Nationalist army in Fukien, late of Shanghai fame, which, in November 1933, revolted and set up a counter-government in Foochow, to which many opponents of Chiang Kai-shek rallied. The Communists refused

to co-operate with these dissidents as being false revolutionaries. It has been suggested that this policy was rejected by Mao Tse-tung.

The question as to what degree Mao, who had been elected Chairman of the Provisional Central Executive Committee of the Kiangsi Soviet Government, was superseded by the men from Shanghai, or whether he was actually for a time openly in opposition to them, remains very obscure. Many records were later lost; others may not háve been allowed to see the light. It is now claimed that Mao was at all times the real leader; but he himself in his writings had pointed out that the mistakes made by others were the cause of the ultimate success of Chiang's Fifth Campaign. The failure to make any accommodation with the Fukien rebels is also claimed to have been contrary to his advice. Clearly, he was not, by his own admission, in full control: or if he was, then the mistakes he identifies were in part at least his responsibility. The weight of evidence in a very obscure question seems to point to a considerable reduction of the power he had wielded before the men from Shanghai reached Juichin. The present mood, in which those who fell from grace in the Cultural Revolution are detected as having been weaker vessels as long ago as 1933-4, does not make the discovery of objective truth any easier.

Chiang's Fifth Campaign

Mao claimed that the leadership in 1933 adopted wrong tactics to meet the formidable menace of the Fifth Extermination Campaign. They fought on fixed positions, and no longer used guerrilla tactics to the full. The real problem is whether, whatever tactics the Communists had adopted, they could in fact have defeated Chiang's assault. He had now at long last learned from his errors, aided by the highly professional advice given him by his new staff of German advisers, lent to him by Hitler, and headed by General von Seeckt (who later commanded the German army in Belgium in the Second World War). Seeckt advised a total blockade of the Communist area. All routes should be shut off, no trade permitted and, as the area is devoid of natural salt supplies, this deprivation would in itself, by spreading disease and deficiency maladies, bring the Communists to surrender. In January 1934 the Fukien revolt had collapsed, and the morale of the Nationalists was raised by this success.

Chiang took his adviser's counsel, and built block houses to constrict the Communist area. He also mounted a massive attack, with over 1,000,000 men and 200 air-

Left: Japanese inspect captured arms after the fall of Mukden, the key city on the Southern Manchurian Railway, in 1931

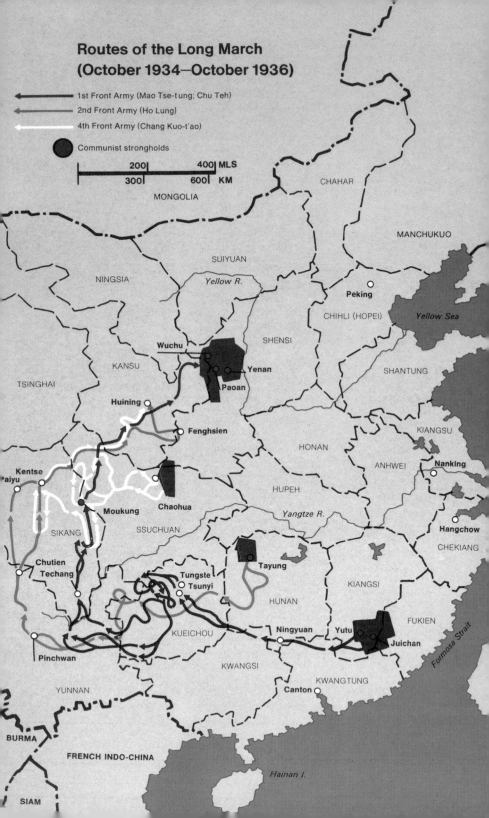

Routes of the Long March
(October 1934—October 1936)

→ 1st Front Army (Mao Tse-tung; Chu Teh)
→ 2nd Front Army (Ho Lung)
→ 4th Front Army (Chang Kuo-t'ao)
● Communist strongholds

| 200 | | 400 | MLS |
| 300 | | 600 | KM |

MONGOLIA

CHAHAR

MANCHUKUO

SUIYUAN

NINGSIA

Yellow R.

Peking

CHIHLI (HOPEI)

Yellow Sea

TSINGHAI

KANSU

Wuchu

SHENSI

Yenan

Paoan

SHANTUNG

Huining

Fenghsien

KIANGSU

Kentse

Paiyu

Moukung

Chaohua

HONAN

ANHWEI

Nanking

SIKANG

SSUCHUAN

Yangtze R.

HUPEH

Hangchow

CHEKIANG

Chutien

Techang

Tayung

Tungste

Tsunyi

KIANGSI

FUKIEN

Pinchwan

KUEICHOU

HUNAN

Ningyuan

Yutu

Juichan

Formosa Strait

YUNNAN

KWANGSI

KWANGTUNG

Canton

BURMA

FRENCH INDO-CHINA

Hainan I.

SIAM

craft—a large force in that period. Whether Mao and Chu, left to their own devices, could have beaten back this attack and broken the blockade must remain unknown. Mao was to state positively that the tactics adopted did not conform with his view, nor with those of Chu Teh. The Returned Students would not trade space for time, as a Nationalist general was later to describe a tactic of the war against Japan. A year later, although they had suffered no disaster, and their resistance to the main assault had cost the Kuomintang dear, the blockade was working too well to be ignored. It was decided to abandon the Kiangsi area, break out, and march across China to the north-west, where a small liberated area—a district under Communist control—had come into existence in northern Shensi. The region was poor but remote; it was also near the frontiers of Mongolia, and could perhaps be seen as on an escape route to Russia. It is doubtful if the Communists really had this in mind.

The Long March

No one has been able to identify the occasion or the men at which and by whom the decision to undertake this epic retreat was made. Mao makes no claim that it was himself, although today all decisions of the past are attributed to him. It does not appear to have been opposed, and the circumstances may have enforced unanimity. In October 1934 about 100,000 fighting men and many women and children broke out from Kiangsi, driving south-west through the lines of provincial troops there charged with maintaining the blockade, and escaping along the mountainous borders of the provinces of Kiangsi, Kuangtung, Hunan and Kuangsi into remote Kueichou. This line of retreat made the most of the traditional lack of co-operation between the forces of one province and its neighbours.

In addition to the main retreat from Kiangsi, the other Communist bases were also abandoned and their defenders undertook separate long marches towards Shensi. The base which had been long established on the borders of Ssuchuan, Hunan, and Hupei, astride the Yangtze, had been commanded by General Ho Lung. He led his men by a route more to the south of that followed by the main army from Kiangsi and, after crossing Hunan and Kueichou, Ho Lung's forces penetrated western and northern Yünnan, crossed the high Yangtze at the small town of Chütien, and struck north through the eastern borders of Tibet. Chang Kuo-t'ao, who had commanded another Communist base in eastern Ssuchuan, moved westward into the mountainous south-western part of that province.

Left: Map showing the progress of the Long March from Kiangsi

All these moves were rarely intercepted or much hindered by the armies of Chiang Kai-shek, who followed the marches, but had not the mobility to catch up with them. Some resistance was met from local warlord armies, especially in Ssuchuan, but for the most part the warlords preferred to defend the cities and leave the Communists to pass through an undefended countryside.

One of the few and most famous engagements was the crossing of the Tatu River in south-west Ssuchuan, a narrow gorge spanned by a chain suspension bridge from which the planks had been removed. An intrepid handful of Communists crossed by swinging hand over hand on the chains, drove off the defenders with hand grenades, and seized the bridge-head. When the various marchers met in Ssuchuan, one of the most crucial disputes in the history of the Party occurred. Chang Kuo-t'ao did not favour the Shensi area for the objective of the retreat; he preferred to continue into Chinese Turkestan, where he expected proximity to the Soviet Union would give protection. Mao upheld the Shensi plan. In the end the two forces separated, Mao and his army crossing the terrible grasslands of eastern Tibet, a high, bleak, infertile and uninhabited region without roads, and finally breaking through opposition to arrive in north Shensi almost exactly one year after his force had left Kiangsi. They had marched about 8,000 miles, and of the 100,000 estimated to have started, not more than 30,000 arrived at the end of the retreat. Most of these losses were due to hardship rather than to enemy action.

Chang Kuo-t'ao crossed and re-crossed the grasslands, but found no means of reaching Sinkiang. He was forced to abandon this objective and join Mao in north Shensi. Ho Lung and the southern marchers also successfully evaded all interception and reached north Shensi. Ho Lung was the last to arrive, nearly one year after the Kiangsi army had reached Shensi. His force raised the combined strength of the Red Armies to 80,000 men. The next year Chang Kuo-t'ao, who had not reconciled himself to Mao's rise to leadership, deserted the cause and sought refuge with the Nationalists. He now lives, an old man, in Hong Kong.

The Long March, or marches, were epic feats of arms, which will be remembered for centuries. But, as Sir Winston Churchill said of Dunkirk, 'a retreat is not a victory'. In terms of military results Chiang Kai-shek could believe that he had gained a great one. He had eliminated all but a small remnant of the **78** ▷

Right: The Battle of Loushan Pass, 1935, which proved to be the turning-point in Communist fortunes. Chiang Kai-shek's forces were routed. Next page: The epic Long March winds across the Great Snow Mountains, a recent painting by Ai Chung-hsin

Communist guerrillas who had for so long defied him in the mountains of south China. He might well think that, weakened and diminished, they could not hold out for long in Shensi, but would be forced to continue their desperate retreat till they crossed into the USSR as many believed they must. He had also won a far greater measure of control over the western provinces, whose warlords, hitherto but very nominal supporters of the Nanking government, had been forced to open their provinces to Chiang's regular armies who were in pursuit of the Red Army. Nanking for the first time gained real power in the south-west, in Ssuchuan and in the north-west, where Muslim generals had long ruled as virtually independent princes.

On the other hand, Chiang had failed to destroy the Red Armies; they had been able to withdraw across the entire length of China by a stupendous march, unharmed by his forces, and had rallied in a new area, just as inaccessible as that from which they had been expelled. It was an area almost impossible to blockade, for it bordered to the north on the empty and inhospitable steppes of western Inner Mongolia. Moreover, the anti-Communist war, and the revolution, had now been carried into northern China, where it had shown few signs of vitality in the past. The northern peasantry, and especially those of the barren north-west, lived under a landlord oppression more harsh even than that of the south; they were a limitless potential for Communist recruitment. North-west China was not a stronghold of the Kuomintang, whereas Kiangsi had been close to Chiang's base areas and region of most strength and support. To carry on the war in north Shensi meant a far greater effort in supply, reinforcement and logistics than the war close to the Yangtze and its tributary rivers in Hunan and Kiangsi.

Chiang Kai-shek's dilemma

There was another difficulty. The Communists had proclaimed that their objective in going north was to prepare to resist the Japanese invasion, which everyone now expected would soon come. The Communists had declared war on Japan. They appealed to the youth of China to support them on patriotic grounds, and used the slogan, soon to be so famous, 'Chinese do not fight Chinese' – a denial of the actual facts of the past twenty years, but an embodiment of the aspiration of the mass of the people.

Chiang still clung to his policy of 'internal pacification before resistance to external aggression'. He continued to hope for diplomatic pressure from the Western powers upon Japan. But those powers, preoccupied by their own impending quarrel with Germany, were in no position to confront Japan in eastern Asia. Instead, they yielded to her at every point. Japanese infringements of foreign

Treaty rights were only met with protests; Japanese occupation of one half of the International Settlement at Shanghai with large forces was not prevented nor resisted. The expansion of Japanese forces in north China, by a gross distortion of the treaty of 1900 — by which the foreign powers had obtained the right to station Legation Guards in Peking and along the railway to the sea, a right in any case obsolete with the removal of the capital to Nanking — amounted to a military occupation of the province of Hopei (in which Peking is situated) and the detachment of its civil government from the direct control of Nanking. All this was causing mounting anger and indignation among the educated class and to some degree among the people also. The open protection which the Japanese gave to the drug traffic in north China was a scandal which roused the fury of many who were by no means willing supporters of the Communists.

Public opinion was beginning to change. Chiang still represented stability to most men; but his foreign policy was under constant and strong criticism. The very fact that the Communists had survived was a point in their favour. Although the real facts of the Long March could not be permitted to be published in Nationalist territory, the extent of the march, the great numbers of people who had seen the Communists at first hand, and the tales they brought of their discipline, endurance and good treatment of the people among whom they had marched, gave a new dimension to the movement which had for so long been represented as 'banditry'. It was also evident, before very long, that far from being crushed, they were, indeed, getting stronger. Chiang's response to this growth of support was to threaten a new series of 'extermination campaigns'. It was not a popular policy. 'Why not fight the Japanese instead?' was a question which found no easy or convincing answer.

Nationalist morale weakens

Gradually the view spread that the continuance of the civil war would benefit no one more (if anyone at all) than the Japanese. They would face a divided China; no adequate military preparation to resist invasion could be made by a government bent on devoting its strength to extermination campaigns which always failed in their objective. Morale among the Nationalists was beginning to be affected by these considerations. Late in 1936, when Chiang was planning a new and powerful extermination campaign, an incident brought the issue to a head.

The Chinese armies of the former warlord of Man-

Left: Chu Teh, a future commander-in-chief of the Red Army, addresses his men during a pause in the Long March

churia, Chang Tso-lin, had come under the command of his son, Chang Hsueh-liang, when the father was assassinated by the Japanese army (as is universally believed) on his withdrawal from Peking in 1928. Two years later, after the younger Chang had intervened, in 1930, to help Chiang crush the rebellion of the northern Nationalists at Peking, the Japanese, who had been displeased by Chang Hsueh-liang's adherence to the Nanking regime, struck in Manchuria and drove the Chinese armies and administration out of the country. Chang Hsueh-liang and his followers became exiles, dependent on Chiang Kai-shek. He took care to move this army away from any region where it might get into contact and conflict with the Japanese, and thus ruin his policy of appeasement. It was finally assigned to the area of south Shensi province, based on Sian, the ancient capital city of the province.

The Manchurian army was to form a major part of the forces engaged on the next extermination campaign. Manchurian soldiers, inured to a cold winter, could stand the climate of Shensi in that season better than the men from the Yangtze area. But the Manchurian troops, and also their comrades, the local Shensi army, were not eager for the fray. They wanted to be led against the Japanese who had taken their country from them. They did not feel any animosity against the Communist forces. They adopted an attitude of passive resistance; they conducted no aggressive actions, they even traded and fraternised with the Communist troops. An unofficial armistice was virtually operating in Shensi by early autumn 1936. Nor was it at all certain that this behaviour by their men was unwelcome to their senior commanders.

The Sian Incident
Chiang Kai-shek was disturbed and alarmed. It was necessary to restore discipline, inspire morale, and urge the reluctant army into action. He decided to visit Sian in person to achieve these objectives. It was too late; the commanders of the Manchurian and Shensi armies had already decided that their men would not fight the Communists and that this must be made plain to the commander-in-chief. They also hoped to force him to change his whole policy and unite the nation for war with Japan.

Chiang paid his first visit to Sian in October 1936. He came to inform his Deputy Commander-in-Chief for Bandit Suppression, i.e. Chang Hsueh-liang himself, that he

Far left: A German jibe at China's 'open door' policy: Japan drives out the Russian bear from Manchuria (top); she is warned that if she wants to play at war she must take care not to get out of hand (bottom). Left: The Red Army at the city gates of Yenan, later to become the Communist headquarters

had completed plans for a new extermination campaign which would be launched early in December. Chang Hsueh-liang responded by urging the head of the Nanking government to change his whole policy, put an end to the civil war, unite the nation in resistance to Japan, and seek alliance with the Soviet Union. This programme bore a striking similarity to that which the Chinese Communist Party, and the Comintern, had proclaimed since 1935. It would seem very probable that it had already been discussed between Hsueh-liang and the emissaries of Mao Tse-tung. Chiang Kai-shek either did not read these signs aright, or chose to ignore them. He abruptly dismissed all such discussion, and reaffirmed his determination to crush the Chinese Communists. Leaving instructions for preparations to go forward he returned to his field headquarters, Loyang, in Honan province.

Intelligence reports must surely have reached him during the next month indicating that his subordinates in Sian were not carrying out their orders with any enthusiasm. There was no evidence of active preparation for offensive action. Once more Chiang decided that his presence was needed, and as he proposed to start the offensive on 12th December, he proceeded to Sian on the 7th to supervise operations. On arrival, he informed his deputy and general, Yang Hu-ch'eng, commanding the local Shensi army, that the offensive would start on 12th December.

Chiang retired for a brief rest to the hot springs situated a few miles outside Sian, a favourite resort of the emperors of the T'ang period. There, on the morning of 12th December, he was arrested by troops under the command of Chang Hsueh-liang and Yang Hu-ch'eng. The two generals had concerted their plans the previous day and the coup was carried out with minimum casualties and disturbance. Chiang Kai-shek was a prisoner. The offensive was called off, and in a telegram addressed to the government in Nanking, Chang and Yang reiterated the programme which Chiang had rejected in October, and made it clear that its acceptance was the price of his life.

The Sian Incident, as it came to be called, made a profound impression. The Nanking government was thrown into disarray; a war party, led by the Chief of Staff Ho Ying-ch'in, wanted to use the air force, assembled for the coming campaign against the Communists, to attack Sian and free the captive head of the Party and State. It is also stated that General Ho got into touch with Wang Ch'ing-wei, Chiang's old opponent within the Nationalist Party,

Left: *The Sian Incident — Chiang Kai-shek (third from right) two days before his capture. The mutineers spared his life on condition that he agreed to resist the Japanese aggressors*

then in Paris, and Wang at once started for China. There can be little doubt that he expected to head the government, with Ho's support, if Chiang met with 'misfortune'.

That this is what would have happened, had the air attack on Sian materialised, is unquestionable. Whatever such an assault might otherwise have achieved, it would have meant the prompt execution of Chiang. Even as things were a strong party of officers in the mutinous army wanted to proceed to this extreme. Madame Chiang (Soong Mei-ling) and her brother, T.V.Soong, Minister of Finance, were completely opposed to such a use of force. Their own position and that of their family — even if no considerations of affection had existed — required that Chiang Kai-shek survive and retain the leadership. It was essential to negotiate with the mutinous generals. Madame Chiang, T.V.Soong, and their Australian adviser, H.Donald, courageously decided to fly to Sian to initiate such negotiations. They no doubt also hoped that their presence in the mutinous camp would inhibit armed attacks upon it.

Chiang's change of mind
They were not the only would-be saviours of Chiang's life to arrive in Sian. He was aided from a most unexpected quarter, the Communist regime in north Shensi, the very enemy he had planned to destroy. Chou En-lai arrived in Sian to persuade the two leaders of the mutiny that the execution of Chiang would be a profound mistake; but that the opportunity for forcing him to renounce his previous policies was unparalleled and might never recur. If Chiang were put to death he would be succeeded by weaker leadership which would break into factions; no decisive change of policy could be expected, and the opportunity for Japan to attack, or impose new servitudes on a distracted China, would enormously increase.

Chang Hsueh-liang and Yang Hu-ch'eng were convinced by this reasoning: so were Madame Chiang and her brother, T.V.Soong. But Chiang Kai-shek, in whose character stubbornness is a dominant trait, refused for long to hear of any such compromise. His whole work would be undone, and perhaps he also saw that the unity of China which could be effected by yielding would at best be short-lived, and might end in a new civil war in which the Communists would be a much more powerful opponent. It cannot yet be known what arguments overcame these doubts. His wife and brother-in-law must have stressed the appalling consequences which would follow his death. Contemplation of his probable successors cannot have been re-

Left: A gathering of the clan — the influential Soong sisters: (from left to right) Mme H.H.Kung, wife of a wealthy financier; Mme Sun Yat-sen; and American-educated Mme Chiang Kai-shek

assuring. But above all it may well have been the fact that national opinion was clearly coming out strongly in favour of a change of policy, and at the same time, in strong support of Chiang himself as the continuing national leader — if only he would agree to lead against the Japanese rather than against his Communist fellow-countrymen.

After two weeks of these persuasions Chiang agreed. He was released on Christmas Day 1936, and flew back to Nanking accompanied by the chief of the mutineers, Chang Hsueh-liang who, with unusual trust and honour in a Chinese of warlord origin, came back to submit to what he no doubt believed would be a face-saving punishment. Instead he was imprisoned, or confined to his house, for the next twenty-seven years.

Chiang had yielded, although no formal document was signed. The Communists were to acknowledge him as head of state and supreme commander of all Chinese armies. They abolished their separate government and renamed their army the 'Eighth Route Army' *(Pa Lu Chun),* a name which, before long, was to be on the lips of every peasant in north China, and acquire lasting fame. In return the Communists retained command of their own forces, and administrative and political control of the 'North-West Border Area', as it was renamed. The ban on the Party was lifted; it became legal to be a Communist. The police terror was ended, and both Parties promised to co-operate in preparing for defence against the threatened Japanese invasion and any further encroachments. The civil war was ended, no further military operations against Communists or Nationalists were to take place. Mao Tse-tung and his administration moved to the city of Yenan, within their area, for the first time occupying a city as their headquarters since the retreat from Juichin in Kiangsi three years before. China was, at last, united. No force in arms against the government remained in the whole country.

The Chinese settle their differences
This result, and the freeing of Chiang Kai-shek, evoked an immense wave of national enthusiasm and relief. Cool heads could no doubt see the flaws in the agreement; and the farsighted could now expect that the Japanese re-action would neither be long delayed nor slight, but to the ordinary man and the newspaper reader, the student and the newly literate city worker, the ending of the civil war was the dawn of a new and better age.

Right: *Chiang Kai-shek (bare-headed) with the ex-Emperor P'u Yi on his right. P'u Yi, deposed in 1911 at the age of six, re-emerged from time to time as the puppet of rival power groups (including, later, the Japanese in Manchuria)*

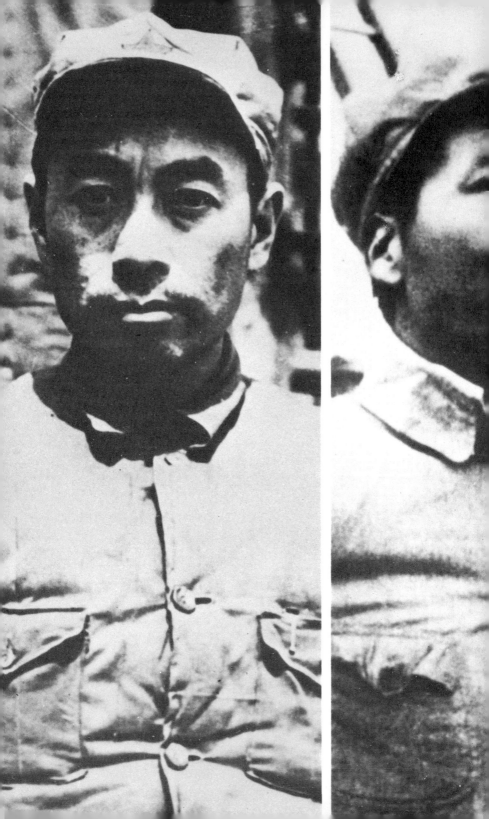

Why, then, had the Communists behaved in what to many seemed a quixotic and incredibly generous manner towards the man who had systematically hunted them down, slain their kinsmen and executed their relatives for ten long years? It must be answered that Mao Tse-tung and his colleagues, with cool calculation, sacrificed their natural feelings of bitterness to what they saw to be the long-term interests of their party and movement.

Chiang Kai-shek, for all his faults, was a national figure; he was the internationally recognised head of the Chinese state. He still commanded the loyalty of millions and would gain still more once he resisted the Japanese: and now he would have to resist them, whether he really wanted to or not. That war was bound to be disastrous, as he well knew: China was weak in comparison to Japan, had no fleet, only a small air force, an army deficient in many modern weapons. Chiang was certain to lose the conventional war against the Japanese army, and with it vast territories. But Mao was also sure that his forces, trained for a decade in guerrilla warfare, and hardened by their tremendous experiences, could, and would, fight the Japanese with equal success. They had no aircraft, but they had never had any; they had no artillery, this too had always been lacking; they did have the expertise to wage a long guerrilla war in difficult country where a modern army, dependent on its large supply train, was at a great disadvantage. The war would last for years, perhaps for a lifetime, but the Communist guerrilla army would emerge at the end as the sole representative of Chinese resistance, and would inherit all power.

The coming war with Japan

For Chiang there was one hope: foreign intervention. He believed, and was to base his whole strategy on the belief, that sooner or later the aggressions of the Japanese and their unbridled ambitions would involve the Western powers, above all the USA. Then China would at last have a reliable ally and against the power of the USA Japan could not, in the end, prevail.

It may be that this view, by hindsight, allows both leaders too much foresight and intuition; Chiang still hoped for foreign intervention before rather than after the Japanese were committed to the invasion of all China. Their manifest ambition, their cavalier treatment of Western foreigners and their treaty rights would never have been tolerated in earlier decades. Nazi Germany, with whom he had good relations, and who had lent him the military advisers who had planned his successful cam-

Left: Two of the earliest and greatest exponents of modern guerrilla warfare—Chou En-lai (far left) and Mao Tse-tung

paign in Kiangsi, was obviously none too enthusiastic a supporter of Japanese policy. He could hope that Hitler would persuade Japan to leave China alone. She had Manchuria, now formed into a puppet 'empire' under P'u Yi, the last Manchu Emperor. Surely that was enough; China would not recognise 'Manchoukuo' as the new state was named, but she neither could nor would be able to do it any harm for very many years, perhaps for ever. If peace could be preserved the Communist objective could be foiled; if they remained in allegiance, they would be confined to a remote, unimportant tract of north-west China. If they broke the peace, they would incur the odium of starting the civil war again, and Chiang could feel confident of national support against them.

These calculations were wrong. Germany did not have that influence over the Japanese military, or if she had any, she did not choose to exercise it decisively. During the subsequent war, before Pearl Harbor, Germany was to try to mediate, but then Chiang Kai-shek, convinced that his hopes lay with the Allied side, would not accept any terms that were offered.

Mao Tse-tung, as a Communist, did not believe that the 'capitalist imperialist' powers could be relied upon; he expected them to make deals between themselves, always at the expense of the Communists. He saw no way of avoiding the coming war, and perhaps did not want to avoid it. His long-term hopes lay in the disruption of the country and its government in the wake of invasion. On the other hand, the more and the longer that the Nationalists actually resisted the Japanese, the weaker they would become, the less able to turn upon the Communists; and they would tie down large Japanese forces. Above all he calculated on the aroused national consciousness of the Chinese people, their endurance and their flexibility, qualities which could be enlisted on a large scale in a massive guerrilla resistance, organised and led by the Communist Party, free from the corruption and nepotism which riddled the Nationalist army and administration.

The three-cornered struggle
The Sian Incident made some stir in the world. It is not every day that the head of a state is made prisoner by mutineers and a long civil war ended to save his life. Yet it is doubtful if the real importance of this event was recognised. It was, as can now be seen, the inevitable prelude to the Japanese invasion. Japan was sadly disappointed. Instead of the China torn by a long civil war, and a government bent on pursuing that conflict instead of preparing resistance to Japanese policies, she found a newly reunited China inspired by an intense emotion of national feeling and patriotism. This was in itself a tire-

some development, but the fact that Chiang had abandoned the anti-Communist campaign largely deprived him of the one value he had had in Japanese eyes.

The Japanese, unlike most of the foreigners in contact with China, did not take the Communists lightly. They were naturally opposed to their social doctrines, but they also saw that they had the potential to win victory in China; and a Communist China, no doubt in close association with Russia, would sound the death knell of Japanese ambitions to carve out an empire on the mainland of Asia. Thus it was necessary to strike first and strike soon, before the Chinese reorganisation could bear fruit.

These views, those of the military party now dominant in Japan, were not wholly shared by their civilian colleagues nor by other important classes of Japanese. There was not the unity of secret and purposeful ambition which outside observers at that time invariably attributed to Japan. The military themselves, divided into different commands, between which were many keen rivalries and jealousies, had no coherent plan of conquest. They wanted to continue the policy of piece by piece encroachment which had paid so well since Manchuria was seized, and seemed to avoid a wholesale confrontation with the entire Chinese people.

None of the participants in the forthcoming struggle truly foresaw its character or its outcome. Chiang was to find that Allied support, although it finally defeated Japan, left him to face an enormously expanded Communist movement. Japan drifted into a vast morass of guerrilla war, in which all her conventional victories achieved no decisive result, and was steadily wearing down her resources. She also provoked the fatal enmity of the USA and brought about her own downfall.

The Communists did not in fact fight on till all Nationalist resistance ceased and they alone became the defenders of China. Before that prospect was even in sight the atomic bombs on Hiroshima and Nagasaki induced the Japanese surrender. The Communist Party found the Nationalists still the recognised government of China, and now that Japan was eliminated, Chiang was once more spoiling for the chance to crush his old enemies. Civil war was to start again, the revolution had taken a long step forward, but it had not yet attained its goal. Yet it can be argued that without the Japanese invasion the Communist conquest of China, if it ever came about, would have taken very many years.

Left: *Pro-Japanese marchers demonstrate against both Chiang Kai-shek and the Communists. Shanghai favoured foreigners*

Chapter 4
Japanese Invasion and Communist Victory

On the night of 7th July 1937, Japanese forces near Peking attempted to enter the small town of Wanping, near the Lukouchiao bridge, a few miles from the city of Peking. The bridge, known to foreigners as the Marco Polo Bridge, because that traveller described it, is an ancient and famous structure; Wanping is the city which guards its southern end. The Chinese garrison resisted, and the Japanese stormed the town. This incident, seemingly deliberately provoked, was the beginning of the Japanese invasion of China.

It was almost exactly ten years since the forces at Nanchang, commanded by Communist officers, had proclaimed themselves to be the Red Army, early in August 1927. In that decade the Communist Party had suffered many changes of fortune, but had emerged at the end in possession of a new sizeable territory in the north-west of the country, had acquired the status of a legal partner in the national government, and rebuilt its strength since the wastage of the Long March. It was now to be exposed to a still greater trial, the full-scale invasion of the armies of a major power. For China the war that began early in July 1937 was not to end for eight years, until the Japanese surrender in August 1945. Few observers would have cared to predict the outcome, but most would have expected a rapid and probably complete Japanese victory.

This expectation seemed at first likely to be fulfilled. The Japanese advance was very swift in north China; Peking was seized on 8th August, Tientsin had already been lost, and the Japanese, previously installed in the northern province of Hopei with Manchuria as their base area, had no difficulty in driving the weak Chinese forces out of the province and then pursuing them into the adjoining regions of Inner Mongolia. Chiang had at first hoped to negotiate another local settlement, but it was soon clear that this was no longer within the scope of Japanese ambitions.

Already, on 28th December 1936, only three days after Chiang had been released at Sian, the Japanese Kuan-

Left: Kuomintang troops go into action wearing German helmets

tung Army (the forces occupying Manchuria) had issued a statement declaring that they supported the policy of their government in seeking co-operation with the Nationalist regime in plans to exterminate the Communists, but that any compromise with the Communists would force Japan to take her own measures. This was a clear enough warning; it was not acceptable to the Chinese. On 15th February 1937, the Central Executive Committee of the Kuomintang meeting at Nanking ratified the agreement which Chiang had been compelled to make with the Communist Party. Throughout the early summer active steps had been taken to prepare for war.

Preparations for war

Chiang Kai-shek was accustomed to make his summer headquarters at the mountain resort of Lushan, near Hankow, above the humid heat of the Yangtze valley. During June he conferred there with the Communist leaders, Mao Tse-tung, Chou En-lai, and their military colleague Chu Teh, commander-in-chief of the Red Army, now renamed the Eighth Route Army. The presence of these senior Communist leaders in the very headquarters of their old foe was a most convincing proof to the Chinese people, and to the Japanese military also, that compromise and indeed co-operation with the Communist Party was now a fact. The conferences were not completed before the Japanese struck at Lukouchiao, and it is hardly in doubt that the Japanese action was spurred on by this clear evidence that their warnings had been rejected. The conference dispersed, the leaders returning to their respective bases, for it was now too late to make contingency plans: the crisis had arrived.

As Japanese advances continued, and no sign of accommodation appeared, the foreign powers were moved to make protests; their own nationals and their property were much in danger. The USA denounced Japanese aggression, but without actually naming Japan, and took no further action. Germany tried to mediate, but made no progress. The Western European powers were at this point too close to war with Germany to risk any involvement in eastern Asia. The USSR, on the other hand, concluded a non-aggression pact with the Nanking government (21st August 1937) and supplied China with a credit of $100,000,000, later adding a further $150,000,000. Large quantities of munitions were transported to China across Siberia and Chinese Turkestan, far from the range of Japanese interference. Five wings of the Soviet air force, with their pilots, were sent to China and took part in the defence of major cities in 1937 and 1938.

Left: *Aftermath of the brutal rape of Nanking by the Japanese*

No doubt this intervention accorded with Soviet policy, but it was nonetheless the only positive aid which China received in her hour of need. It served to strengthen the claim of the Communist Party that all the capitalist-imperialist powers were unreliable friends, and that only the USSR could be trusted. One consequence was that on the distant frontiers of Japanese Manchoukuo (Manchuria) and Outer Mongolia, which was a client state of the Soviet Union, violent frontier clashes occurred both in July/August 1938 and the next year, between May and August 1939 at Nomonhan, in the same region. In both actions the Japanese had attempted, with success at first, to take strong positions within what the Russians regarded as their territory or that of Outer Mongolia. On both occasions the Russians brought up strong forces and then struck back with complete success. In the second clash at Nomonhan 30,000 Japanese and about an equal force of Soviet troops were engaged. The Japanese losses were very heavy, and no further attempts at probing the Russian positions followed. Marshal Zhukov, later of Stalingrad fame, was the Russian commander.

The Japanese offensive
Elsewhere, against poorly armed Chinese troops, the Japanese had more success. They had overrun all Inner Mongolia by October 1937, and had invaded the province of Shansi, west of Peking. Here they met, for the first time, Communist forces in strength who were holding the pass at Pinghsingkuan, guarding the approach to the provincial capital. The Communists put up a strong resistance, and delayed the Japanese for several days. But outnumbered and outflanked, they then had to withdraw into the mountains. Japanese forces occupied Taiyuan, capital of the province, on 9th November. They had also pushed southward into northern Honan and to the borders of Shantung, but halted there; as it proved, because they were in secret negotiations with a treacherous Nationalist general, Han Fu-chu, who commanded in that province.

In August 1937 the war had also spread to central China, the Japanese using the eastern half of the International Settlement at Shanghai to launch another invasion. It was very strongly opposed by the regular Chinese army for over three months, a feat which at the time caused amazement in the world at large, where the fighting capacity of Chinese troops was rated low. By a further landing near Hangchou the Japanese outflanked

*Right: Japanese troops overrun a key railway junction near Hsuchow. **Far right:** Map showing the Communist advance in China **(top)**; the triumphal entry of the Japanese army into Nanking still did not lead to Chinese submission **(bottom)***

Communist Front, 1947
Communist Front, 1948
Communist Front, 1949
Communist Front, 1950

USSR

MONGOLIA

MANCHURIA
Controlled by Russia 1945-48
by China from 1948

KOREA

Changchun

Mukden

Antung

Tientsin
Peking

Yenan
Communist
stronghold
from 1936

Taiyuan
Tsinan
Tsingtao
Loyang
Sian
Yungcheng
Nanking

TIBET

Yellow R.

Wuhan
Hangchow
Shanghai

Chungking

Yangtze R.

INDIA

BURMA

FRENCH
INDO-CHINA

Canton

TAIWAN
(FORMOSA)

SIAM

Hainan I.

福
建

the defenders of Shanghai and compelled them to fall back
on Nanking. Using their naval forces on the Yangtze,
which China could not effectively oppose, the Japanese
took Nanking itself in mid-December, and then sullied
the reputation of their army by permitting an unre-
strained sack and massacre, which the world press
stigmatised as 'The Rape of Nanking'.

Another landing in the far south near Hong Kong had
resulted in the capture of Canton on October 21st. As
many believed, the feeble Chinese resistance there, in
striking contrast to the defence of Shanghai, betokened
further treachery. This evil was openly apparent when
the Shantung general Han Fu-chu abandoned Tsinan,
capital of his province, without resistance. He withdrew
south, but Chiang still had the power to have him arrested,
brought to Wuhan, the temporary capital, and there shot.

The Japanese had expected a Chinese overture for peace
after the fall of Nanking — were they not proving irresis-
tible? — but no such offer came in the winter months, and
therefore in spring 1938 the Japanese resumed their advance southward from Shantung. In this unusual war,
marred by treachery and cowardice in some cases, but
illuminated by courage and endurance in others, the
Japanese were now to encounter the second situation.

Moving south from Tsinan to take the important railway junction of Suchou, where the north-south Tientsin-
Nanking railway crosses the east-west Lunghai railway,
the Japanese met with a considerable disaster at the
small village of Taierhchuang, losing nearly two divisions.
The Chinese commander of this, almost the only successful field action of the war, was Li Tsung-jen, a Kuangsi
general, later to be last vice-president of Nationalist
China, and still later to rally to the Communist side.

The Japanese were nevertheless able, by advancing
from Nanking in the south, to take Suchou, and then
turned west along the Lunghai railway. Kaifeng, capital
of Honan, was taken in May, but at this point Japanese
strategy was frustrated by the Chinese action in breach-
ing the dykes of the Yellow River, which thereupon
changed its course, flowed south-east instead of north-
east, and spread a vast destructive flood in the path of the
Japanese advance. It destroyed a huge region, led to the
death of thousands of peasants, eliminated cities and villages, and even twenty years later, in 1956, the area was
only just once more becoming habitable under the in-
tensive restoration programme carried out by the new
Communist government. This was, indeed, the 'scorched
earth' policy which China had proclaimed to be her
answer to Japanese invasion.

Left: Soldiers and peasants are urged to fight Japan, 1938

99

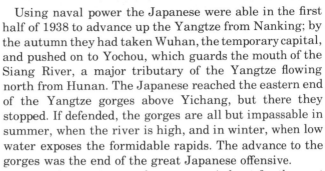

Using naval power the Japanese were able in the first half of 1938 to advance up the Yangtze from Nanking; by the autumn they had taken Wuhan, the temporary capital, and pushed on to Yochou, which guards the mouth of the Siang River, a major tributary of the Yangtze flowing north from Hunan. The Japanese reached the eastern end of the Yangtze gorges above Yichang, but there they stopped. If defended, the gorges are all but impassable in summer, when the river is high, and in winter, when low water exposes the formidable rapids. The advance to the gorges was the end of the great Japanese offensive.

No further major attacks were carried out for the next six years. The Japanese had already discovered that rapid advances along main lines of communication might eliminate the regular Chinese troops, but left the invaders with a vast task of occupation and pacification in the great areas served by no modern communications of any kind. It was in these areas that the Communist armies began to operate with increasing effect from the end of 1937.

The Japanese occupation

The Japanese could not believe that the huge losses of territory, the very heavy casualties they had inflicted — 800,000 in their estimate for a cost of only 50,000 of their own — would not compel Chiang Kai-shek to seek peace. They had induced his old opponent, Wang Ch'ing-wei, to carry their terms to Chungking, Chiang's wartime capital in Ssuchuan, on 18th December. They amounted to the acceptance of a Japanese protectorate in fact if not in name, and full co-operation with the Japanese to destroy the Communist armies and movement. The Japanese offered no terms to Mao Tse-tung.

On 26th December 1938 Chiang Kai-shek publicly rejected the Japanese overtures; Wang Ch'ing-wei then left Chungking, made his way to French Indo-China through Yünnan, and soon after defected to the Japanese, who made him the head of their puppet government installed at Nanking. Wang died in office there, before the Japanese surrender.

If Chiang would not make peace, he equally had no real intention of carrying on active war. He believed, rightly, that sooner or later the Japanese would come into conflict with the USA, and that then the war would be as good as won. He planned to foster his strength to deal with the Communist movement when Japan was eliminated. He is quoted as having said, at about this time, that 'the Japanese are a disease of the skin; the Communists a disease of the heart'. Whether true or not, these words aptly summarise his inner convictions. He still controlled

Left: The massive bombardment of Chungking, September 1940

101

western China, the large provinces of Ssuchuan, Shensi (apart from the Communist region in the north), western Honan, above the Yellow River rapids, Kansu and the far north-west, Hunan, Yünnan, Kueichou, and Kuangsi in the south. Parts of the coastal provinces of Kuangtung and Fukien were still in his occupation. This was in itself a great state, but cut off at all points from the sea. Communication with the outer world could only be effected by land through Yünnan or Burma, or by air over the same route, or across the far north-west by Sinkiang to Russian Central Asia. Almost all the modern industry of China was in Japanese hands; the western provinces were agriculturally rich in some areas, but undeveloped, without communications, and still functioning on an almost wholly pre-industrial economy.

The Japanese, in addition to Manchuria, had overrun and occupied Hopei, Shansi, Shantung, Anhui, Kiangsu, Kiangsi, Hupei, and part of Honan. They also held the essential ports in the southern provinces of Chekiang, Fukien and Kuangtung. In very rough terms the Japanese had occupied the eastern half of China; Chiang still held the western half. But Japanese occupation was everywhere thin. The region overrun was huge, corresponding to Europe west of Russia. Very few main-line railways crossed it, the navigable Yangtze was the only major means of communication in the centre, the sea the only link with the southern enclaves. Japan controlled the sea, and the Yangtze also with her unchallenged Navy. But in the vast rural interior of north and north-central China, the Navy could not operate, and the guerrillas could. Nationalist efforts to organise guerrilla resistance in the northern and central provinces were few and unsuccessful. They had no trained fighters to form a core of experienced men. The Communist army was, on the other hand, made up of precisely this type of soldier.

Peasant support for the Communists

As the Nationalist armies withdrew or dispersed, the Eighth Route Army and its ever increasing militia—made up of local peasants who fought only in their own district —spread and infiltrated the countryside. They operated close to great cities; the Western Hills, in sight of Peking, were a continuing stronghold, and others were active in the lake country a few miles from Shanghai. They also penetrated the wild and steep mountains, which had no roads fit for vehicles, and above all they were secretly present in the innumerable villages of the plains, which

Right: War spared nobody. Disease, starvation, and Japanese planes caused havoc among fleeing civilians. Here a mother grieves for her son, injured by a fall from a packed refugee train

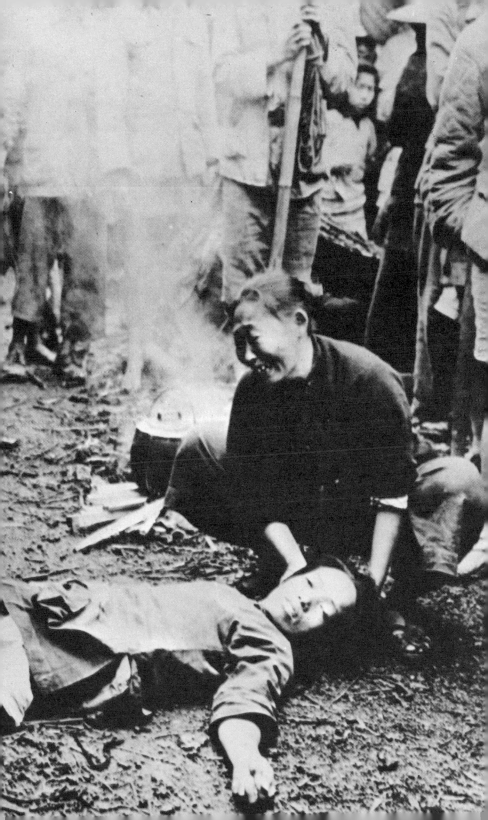

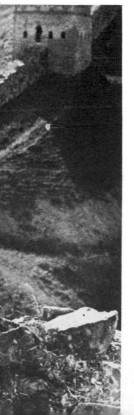

at intervals of barely a mile or less dot the great eastern flat lands of Honan, southern Hopei, western Anhui, and Shantung. The population here is thick; each village much resembles the next; there was no way, without actual patrol contact, for the Japanese to know whether this or that village was a guerrilla stronghold. Japanese patrols, making their way along the dusty tracks which served for roads, were easily detected in advance. The guerrillas disappeared.

This type of resistance was made possible only by the co-operation of the peasants. They gave information to the guerrillas, denied it to, or misled the invaders. They fed the guerrilla formations, carried their messages, hid them, and provided them with clothing, the rough peasant garments made in the villages themselves. The Communist guerrillas, to survive, had to win peasant support and hold it; they had to offer the peasants an alternative better than compliance with Japanese orders.

As a political task this was a formidable assignment. In a great part of the region, indeed in the vastly preponderant part, the Communists had never operated before. They were unknown, strangers, some even southerners, whose dialect was hard to follow. At any other period they would have met with no response from the north Chinese peasant. He was not politically conscious; he knew, and loathed, the military forces of his own government which had for so many years battened on him, stolen his crops, and squeezed out his scarce money. He was instinctively hostile to all armies. Republic or monarchy meant little to him; the emperor was gone, he knew, and chaos and misgovernment had been his visible successors. Now came the Japanese and the guerrillas; what was there to choose between them?

It was perhaps a decisive factor in the success of the Communists that the Japanese themselves provided the conclusive answer to this question. They felt themselves alien in a hostile, or at least an unco-operative land. They tried to enforce obedience, to organise the countryside for their benefit. These measures interfered with peasant ways, and cut across the traditional laisser-faire of Chinese government.

The Japanese are a highly disciplined people; they do what they are told. The Chinese peasant is not a disciplined man; he does what he always traditionally did, that and no more, unless he is shown very good reason and personal advantage to do otherwise. In later times Mao and the Communist Party themselves were to find this ancient characteristic a serious impediment to their poli-

Top left: *Advancing Japanese cavalry.* **Bottom:** *A section of the Red Army on duty on a stretch of the Great Wall of China*

cies. In Japan, if you disobeyed the police you were sure of serious trouble. In China, either you bribed the policeman, or intimidated him through the force of your kinsmen and fellow villagers.

The Japanese did not understand this significant difference. They gave orders, and when they were disobeyed, or evaded, then they punished. The Chinese retaliated when they could, they were then given more severe punishment, villages were fined or otherwise penalised. When the guerrillas appeared and told the peasants that this was what they must expect from imperialist conquerors they found an audience. When the guerrillas grew strong enough to hinder Japanese patrols, drive out their police, or even interrupt roads and railways with demolition raids, the peasants began to take notice. The Communists did not loot, they did not steal food, they paid for what they needed, they brought some medical help to the villages and taught the young what the war was about.

Resistance and reprisals

The Japanese found that the countryside was turning hostile, not merely indifferent. The remedy seemed to be the creation of puppet Chinese governments, and a puppet, Japanese-trained police force and local military units. The difficulty was to get any men of probity and value to man these organisations. Venal former politicians were to be found to staff government offices in Peking or Nanking, doing very little for what pay they got. In the country, local bullies, the tough village bad hats who had always been at the disposal of landlords, could be induced to head local police units and militia. But these were the very people whom the Chinese peasantry had hated and feared for generations. They were now identified with the invader, so the people turned to the guerrillas, who were the only remedy. Repression, retaliation, further repression, fiercer retaliation, became the terrible rhythm of life in the occupied areas. Before two years or so had passed the Japanese were fighting a 'dirty war' in the very fullest sense of that term in every occupied province.

To the Communists it was not the war with Japan — that term did not suit their propaganda. It was the 'War of Resistance' — as it is still known — and resistance was to 'imperialism' and 'feudalism', whether Japanese, puppet, or inevitably, before very long, Nationalist also.

From the point of view of the Communist Party and the guerrilla forces, what went on in the Nationalist part of China, or beyond China, was almost wholly irrelevant. Their war was a local one, fought with deadly hatred and cold courage in a thousand villages, and it was socially disruptive.

To understand why China became a Communist coun-

try, the nature of the guerrilla war is the essential clue. It ruined the old order. Typical of many hundreds of villages and small towns all over this region, was the history of a place called Hsu Shui, not more than twenty miles from the large city of Paoting in Hopei, and on the Peking-Hankow railway. Hsu Shui, its inhabitants now relate, was 'liberated' twenty-seven times in the eight years' war. By this they mean that twenty-seven times the guerrillas took the little town – or its ruins – and twenty-six times the Japanese sallied out of Paoting and drove them away. Meanwhile every inhabitant except the very poor had fled; the land was left uncultivated, except the best, which the survivors tilled in common. The guerrillas taught them how to make rifles and ammunition, armed them and organised them in a secret militia.

When the war ended only these dedicated men remained in the place, and they were whole-hearted supporters of the Communist Party. They run it still. The war itself had created a social revolution which no restoration could undo without a further bloodbath.

These were the reasons, and the steps by which, in the years of resistance, the Communists won their great support, and expanded their 'liberated areas'. These districts, usually centred on some difficult piece of terrain, were wholly free from Japanese control; in other places the Japanese or their puppets might appear by day, but the guerrillas ruled by night.

Japanese repression, Communist gain

In 1942 the Japanese launched a major offensive called the 'Three All Campaign'; i.e. 'Burn All, Loot All, Kill All'. The peasants of villages which had, or were suspected of having, supported the guerrillas, were to suffer these things. No great effort was made to distinguish which they were. The Communists have admitted suffering great losses at this time. Their active force was heavily engaged and much reduced, the liberated areas were sometimes overrun, or greatly constricted. But the offensive failed. It could not be kept up, the area was too great. The consequences were to drive thousands of refugee peasants into the arms of the Communists, and these men who had seen their villages destroyed and their kin slain, who had lost everything, were the best possible and the most ardent recruits the Communists could enlist. The effect, as seen in the last three years of the war, was to consolidate, and then to expand, the Communist strength and control over still larger areas and many more millions of people.

Left: There was no peace for the Japanese once the peasants had been organized into a hostile and effective guerrilla force

After the early active phase of the war, in which the Nationalist armies had been driven back into western China, the relations between Nationalists and Communists began to deteriorate. One reason for this was undoubtedly the fact that guerrilla resistance in occupied territory was coming under exclusive Communist control and direction. This could mean – and in fact was destined to mean – a vast increase in the following and support of the Communist Party, a prospect very unwelcome to Chiang Kai-shek.

Nationalist treachery

In October 1940 an incident in central China demonstrated all too clearly how bad relations were becoming. The Communists had revived their guerrillas and more regular forces in the mountain and lake area west of Shanghai and south of Nanking, a region in which they had never been active on a large scale before the war. This new army was called the New Fourth Army, and was establishing a stronghold in the south-east, the area which in peacetime was the real base and homeland of Chiang's regime. As commander-in-chief of all Chinese armies Chiang now ordered the New Fourth Army to cross to the north bank of the Yangtze. This was, in any case, an order which must have seemed questionable to the Communists. The Yangtze was patrolled by strong Japanese naval forces, and in its lower course below Nanking is often as much as two miles in width, widening still more as it draws closer to the sea. To cross this obstacle in the presence of hostile naval forces was most hazardous. It cannot have seemed improbable that Chiang was inviting the New Fourth Army to an act of suicide.

There were still Nationalist forces in the parts of Anhui and Kiangsu on the south bank of the river. It was claimed that these would take over from the New Fourth Army in the region. The Communists therefore reluctantly agreed to cross to the north bank, and carried out this dangerous manoeuvre in the only possible way, secretly, and in small detachments, by night. More than two-thirds of the army had safely crossed when the remaining detachments and the headquarters itself, which was still on the south bank, were suddenly attacked by Nationalist forces in greatly superior strength and virtually wiped out. The chief-of-staff was killed, his deputy wounded and made prisoner. There can be no question that this onslaught was most treacherous and

Far left: America provides military aid to China: the Burma Road *(top)* was the lifeline along which supplies to Chiang Kai-shek's army flowed; General Stilwell, chief of staff to Chiang Kai-shek, supervises the instruction of Chinese troops in India *(bottom). Left:* The Red Army advances under a pall of smoke

109

unprovoked. It caused a wave of shock and resentment, and was observed with alarm by China's friends abroad.

Chiang, realising that either his subordinates had exceeded orders — as was claimed — or that the reaction to his orders was much stronger than he had anticipated, made efforts to disclaim responsibility. The affair was not allowed to develop into an open breach, the New Fourth Army moved away into central China — Japanese-occupied areas — but the agreement and co-operation inaugurated after the Sian Incident was fatally impaired.

Japan on the defensive

Within a year of this clash the Japanese assault on Pearl Harbor gave Chiang what he had always hoped for — the alliance of the USA and the certainty of ultimate victory. Even though the early course of the Pacific War was so disastrous to the Allies he never wavered in this belief. After the war would be the time to settle the question with the Communists, now they could be left to keep the Japanese busy while he husbanded his strength.

There were no more open clashes with Communist forces; instead, Chiang deployed up to half a million of his best-equipped men — soon to be armed with American weapons — not to fight the Japanese, as the Americans expected, but to form a *cordon sanitaire* shutting off the north Shensi border area, the Communist base region, from all contact with Nationalist China. No American entreaties or persuasions were ever able to alter this strategy. The Nationalist armies did not engage the Japanese, nor did they attack the Communists, they simply blockaded the border between their own territory and that of the Communist regional regime. Not even medical supplies subscribed for by foreign aid organisations were permitted to reach Yenan. It needed no prophet to see that if Japan were defeated, a new civil war in China was most probable.

This situation persisted throughout the Pacific War. The Nationalist armies were inactive, the regime became rotten with corruption and nepotism; the guerrilla war continued, and after 1942 the Japanese were progressively forced on to the defensive in the Pacific War, and no longer free to apply maximum pressure in China. Their hold on the occupied areas began to weaken. Late in 1944, the Japanese did renew their offensive against the Nationalists in south-east China to destroy the air bases which the Americans had built and from which they mounted destructive raids on Japanese shipping. This

Left: Communist troops ride through the night. The civil war that had never really stopped since 1928 was resumed in 1946

111

offensive brought the Japanese deep into southern China and eliminated the bases most useful to the US Air Force.

The resistance of the Nationalist armies was feeble. The campaign did not increase Chiang's standing in the eyes of his Allies, but the war was now going hardly against Japan and Germany; victory was not far away. Neither Communists nor Nationalists foresaw how it would so suddenly end.

The defeat of Germany clearly put still greater pressure on Japan; but everyone expected that the Japanese, inspired by their fanatical patriotism, would defend their country inch by inch, if invaded, and cling to their conquests abroad with equal tenacity. The atomic bombs on Hiroshima and Nagasaki, totally unexpected by Chinese of all parties, altered everything. Within days Japan had unconditionally surrendered. The expected American invasion of eastern occupied China never took place.

At the Japanese surrender the military and political balance between the Communists and Nationalists had changed out of all recognition from what it had been in 1937. The Communist Party now counted 1,210,000 members; it had a regular army of 910,000 men and a militia, serving locally, of 2,200,000. It ruled a population of 95,500,000. The Japanese 'occupied' territories comprised 914 county towns, and of these, by the spring of 1945, no less than 678 were in Communist hands. This was, therefore, the confrontation of two major powers.

MacArthur recognises Chiang

The Nationalist armed forces were even larger, in proportion of about five to one, but this figure applied only to the regular armies. The Nationalists had also a monopoly of heavy weapons and equipment, and an air force which was supreme, since the Communists had no aircraft. The immediate question arose: which army should accept the surrender of the Japanese garrisons, and acquire their large stocks of weapons and supplies? The Communists claimed the right to take surrenders in all areas where they dominated the countryside. Chiang Kai-shek forbade this, and ordered the Japanese garrisons to hold their positions until his own men could arrive to take over. On 15th August, the day after the Japanese surrender, General MacArthur, supreme Allied commander in the Pacific, authorised Chiang Kai-shek, as acknowledged supreme commander of the China war zone, to take the surrenders, and put the US transport air force at his disposal to fly his men to the isolated cities held by the Japanese. This was the immediate cause of

Right: Mao's army on the move after the Japanese surrender

the last great civil war. The USA felt itself legally obliged to take this course on behalf of the legal recognised government of China. The Communist side saw these acts as a breach of faith; they promptly cut the main line railways and thus denied all land communication between central and north China.

The US authorities and administration hoped at all costs to prevent a further Chinese civil war. General George Marshall was sent to China to mediate and, if possible, contrive a peaceful settlement. He was able to arrange a ceasefire in January 1946 while negotiations were pursued in Chungking, and later in Nanking, for a coalition government. Mao Tse-tung briefly visited Chungking, and Chou En-lai remained there as chief Communist delegate. Neither side trusted the other, and the efforts of third parties, both American and Chinese, were of no avail. The Communist side demanded a complete democratisation of the government; Chiang had no intention of really surrendering his dictatorial power. All hope of peace vanished as a result of developments in Manchuria. Russia had occupied that country in a swift campaign waged after the atomic bombs had already fallen on Japan. The Soviet Union took the surrender of the Japanese army in Manchuria, and agreed to withdraw from the country by January 1946. The question which then arose was who would subsequently occupy these rich provinces, which the Japanese had developed more than any other region in China. The Communists had already infiltrated 130,000 men, as the Russians did not occupy the countryside. The Communists also found large stocks of Japanese weapons and enlisted men from the disbanded puppet army of defunct 'Manchoukuo', who were local Chinese, and had had military training. Chiang determined to take over the country as the Russians went out, by force if necessary. It was this question which ruined the truce. Fighting in Manchuria began late in 1945 and did not cease until the Communist conquest was complete.

The civil war resumes

While Chiang had his American-trained and equipped elite troops, who were stationed in the far south-west of the country adjoining Burma at the surrender, transported by sea to Manchurian ports, the Communists set up a strong blocking force at Ssupingkai, a city on the railway from Mukden to the north of Manchuria. This held up the Nationalist advance, and behind it the Communists were able to take over the whole of the most northerly province of Manchuria, Heilungkiang, from the

Right: Red troops attack a Nationalist-held town in Manchuria

114

Russians when they completed their evacuation in May 1946. The subsequent efforts of the Nationalists succeeded in regaining some cities, including Changchun, the former capital of Manchoukuo, and the ports on the gulf of Liaoning, but they were never able to enter northern Manchuria. It remains an interesting fact that although the Communist Party from early in 1946 controlled Heilungkiang province, which borders on Soviet Siberia, and had the peaceful occupation of Harbin, a great industrial city, they did not set up their administration there, nor centre their regime on this protected province, so close to Russian territory. They moved their headquarters from Yenan into eastern China, but not to north Manchuria.

By June 1946 the truce in China within the Great Wall also collapsed and full-scale civil war resumed. General Marshall went home declaring that the fault for his failure to mediate lay with both parties in equal measure.

The Nationalist strategy, apart from the attempt to occupy Manchuria, was directed to reopening railway communications between the Yangtze valley, which they held, and their north China garrisons in Peking, Tientsin, and some lesser cities. This would also give them direct land communications with Manchuria. The Communists were prepared to sacrifice their old strongholds in the north-west, no longer of major strategic importance, in order to deny the Nationalists passage to the north. The struggle therefore centred on the province of Shantung, through which passes the most direct railway link between Nanking and north China. It later spread to the areas crossed by the Peking-Hankow railway, the second link between north and south.

The Nationalists begin to give way

In 1946 the Nationalists failed to conquer Shantung and open the railway. Indeed they suffered heavy losses in the attempt. Early in 1947 they compensated for this significant failure by scoring the apparent victory of occupying Yenan, the old Communist capital in the northwest. However, Yenan was not defended, and the Nationalist campaign in the north-west was a decoy which drew their strength away from the vital eastern battlefronts. Later, in August, the futility of this north-western foray was illustrated by the Communist counter-offensive in central China which established them in Hupei province, close to Wuhan, and thus threatened the Nationalist flank. In the same summer they finally drove the Nationalists out of Shantung and frustrated the attempt to open railway communication with the north. By the end of 1947 the civil war had taken a definite turn in favour of the Communists; the possibility of outright victory re-

garded in 1945 as hardly possible, was now becoming real.

Communist military progress was helped by the progressive deterioration of the Nationalist regime. A wild inflation had destroyed the value of the currency; corruption was flagrant and open, morale was falling, the oppressive police repression in the name of anti-Communism was taking victims, usually men of liberal views, and creating an atmosphere of fear and despair in all classes. The top members of the regime, including the family and in-laws of the leader, were notoriously enriching themselves by manipulation of the exchanges, appropriation of so-called enemy property (any property which the Japanese had seized) and other devices. American advice to Chiang to change his ways, democratise and reorganise his regime, and enforce honesty in his army and administration went unheeded. His position depended on a network of loyalties each of which required satisfaction in terms of power and wealth; he could not break out of a system which had grown for twenty years.

By contrast the people of China were now able to see in the Communist armies, as they advanced, a superbly disciplined force, which neither looted, nor raped, nor was even allowed to commandeer food or lodging without payment. No corruption marred its administration, efficiency was evident, dedication apparent. It might well be that these qualities covered others which would not be so welcome to all classes in time to come, but few people, after the horrors and deprivations of the past decade, cared for the more distant future. The universal demand was for peace now; soon it was to favour any sort of peace, and this meant Communist victory.

The Communists move into the open

The year 1948 brought this very much nearer. In the early months the Communists scored a series of stunning victories in Manchuria which reduced the Nationalist hold on the country to its two largest cities, Mukden (Shenyang) and Changchun. Very large Nationalist forces were besieged in these places and, unless relieved, could not hold out beyond the summer. Chiang made a supreme effort to achieve this aim, but as he had no communications except by sea with Manchuria, it took him most of the summer months to build up strength. Meanwhile his position in central China continued to decline.

In April 1948 the Communists overran the province of Honan and, in September, carried the city of Tsinan,

Left: *Manchurians from Lin Piao's Communist columns enter ancient Peking. Chanting their three commandments — 'Do not take even a needle or thread. Consider the people as your family. All that you have borrowed you must return' — they did not conform to the popular picture of a conquering army*

capital of Shantung, by direct assault. This was the first large city in China within the Great Wall which the Communists permanently occupied. Its fall was generally seen as a portent. It is believed that its capture signified an important change of strategy and tactics; guerrilla war had served its turn, the Communist armies were now strong enough to confront the Nationalists in conventional battles, and make permanent conquests of large cities. It was also believed in Peking at that time that this policy was adopted in contradiction to the advice of Stalin, who wanted a prolonged war which he believed would involve America in defence of Chiang Kai-shek. The Chinese Communists on the other hand saw China's interests as lying in a quick decision before American alarm at the decline of the Nationalists could crystallise into a policy of intervention.

The historic encounter of Huai Hai

Two great victories decided the issue of the civil war. In October 1948 Lin Piao, Communist commander in Manchuria, totally routed the Nationalist armies trying to relieve Mukden, and then destroyed the great garrison of that city itself. It surrendered on 29th October with a Nationalist loss of nearly 500,000 men, for the most part prisoners of war. Changchun had also capitulated with its garrison of five divisions and all their equipment. Manchuria was wholly in Communist hands. Inevitably freed from this preoccupation, they turned their full strength south and met the last stand of the Nationalists near Suchou, the railway junction on the Lunghai and Tientsin-Nanking railways, in the valley of the Huai river. The great decisive battle is therefore known to the Chinese by the contraction 'Huai Hai', i.e. Huai River and Lung Hai railway. The rival forces were approximately equal in number, about 600,000 on each side. The Nationalists still had air support, the Communists did not but, after the massive losses in equipment in Manchuria, the weapons on either side were more equal. Chiang had ordered his forces to hold Suchou at all costs, as it is the gateway to the south and its loss would imperil Nanking itself. The region has, from ancient times, been the site of the great battles between dynasties based in the south and their rivals from the north; it is the natural passage between north and central China.

The Nationalists lost the battle of Huai Hai for the same reasons that they had been defeated in Shantung, Central China, and Manchuria: bad leadership, inflexible tactics, inability to match their opponents' mobility, and the loss of morale among their own men. Whole

Left: Eve of victory — Nationalists surrender at bayonet point

units, regiments, even divisions surrendered. The battle of Huai Hai, the greatest engagement ever fought in Chinese history, and one which rivals in the numbers of those involved any of the major battles of our own or previous ages, was very little understood or noticed in the world at large. The Chinese civil war was so old a news story that it no longer rated major headlines.

Yet it was one of the decisive battles; after it the Nationalist Party had lost the war; it could only hope to negotiate a surrender which would leave it a nominal existence. Chiang Kai-shek withdrew from the Presidency, and later went to Taiwan (Formosa), to which island he was able to bring several thousands of his remaining troops and those commanders who were most loyal to him. The Nanking government under its provisional President, Li Tsung-jen, spent the first four months of 1949 in negotiations with Peking, now the Communist headquarters (it had surrendered after six weeks' siege in January 1949). However, these negotiations were ended by the intervention of Chiang's supporters; the Communists resumed the war in April 1949, crossed the Yangtze and took Nanking, then advanced and took Shanghai in May and, by the end of the year, had taken over all south, central and western China.

On 1st October 1949 the Peoples' Republic of China was proclaimed in Peking, which became once more the capital of China. The war was over, except for the residual hold of the Nationalists upon Taiwan and some small islands nearer to the mainland. It was twenty-two years since the division under Chu Teh proclaimed itself to be the Red Army in August 1927, and twenty-one years since he and Mao Tse-tung first organised a Communist administration on Chingkangshan Mountain in Kiangsi. Now they controlled all China. In the sense of armed struggle the Revolution was over, victory had conclusively gone to the Communists, and no future development for very many years, perhaps centuries, is likely to alter this result. The regime may undergo internal changes and is indeed doing so, but these take place within the system that Mao has created. The rise of the Chinese Communist Party and its triumph thus constitutes one of the most significant events in the modern history of the world.

Right: The seal of victory — Mao Tse-tung proclaims the Peoples' Republic of China in Peking on 1st October 1949, a momentous occasion which today's visitors to the Museum of Chinese Revolution in Peking can relive at leisure (**far right**)

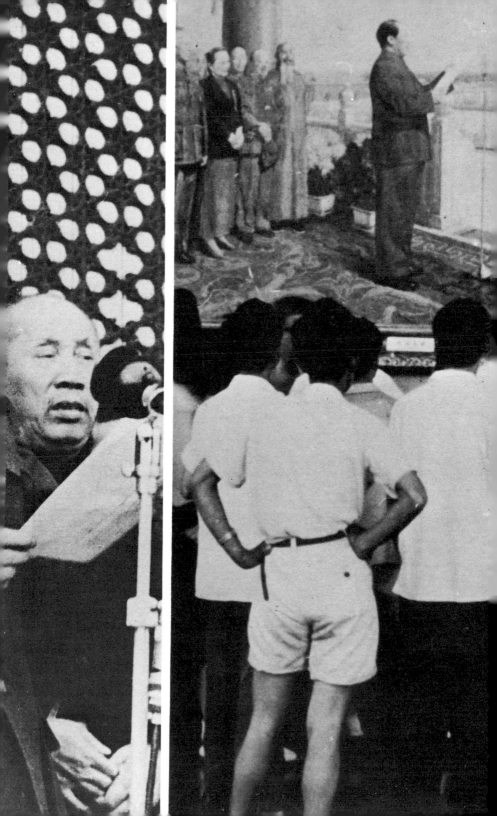

Chronology of Events

1839 **November:** the First Opium War breaks out. It is ended by the
1842 Treaty of Nanking which is signed on 29th August 1842
1850 The T'ai P'ing Rebellion breaks out
1858 **26th-29th June:** the treaties of Tientsin are signed between China and Great Britain, France, the United States, and Russia
1894 The Sino-Japanese war exposes China's frailty
1898 **11th June-16th September:** the Hundred Days of Reform
1900 The Boxer Rebellion, encouraged by an anti-foreign Manchu clique. **14th August:** Peking is taken and the Court flees (15th).
1911 **10th October:** the outbreak of the Chinese Revolution—Yüan Shih-k'ai is given full military and political authority
1912 **12th February:** the Manchu dynasty abdicates, setting up by imperial decree a republic as its successor. Yüan Shih-k'ai is elected provisional president and Sun Yat-sen resigns
1915 **18th January:** Japan presents to China her Twenty-One Demands
1916 **6th June:** Yüan Shih-k'ai dies. The Warlord Era begins
1917 Sun Yat-sen rallies the republican faithful at Canton but his regime is overthrown in 1918
1919 **May:** students demonstrate in Peking; on the 4th, houses of corrupt ministers are burnt and their cars destroyed. **28th June:** the Chinese delegation refuses to sign the Treaty of Versailles
1920 Civil war reigns throughout China, destroying national unity
1921 The Chinese Communist Party is founded at a secret meeting in the French Concession of Shanghai

1924 **21st January:** the first Kuomintang national congress is held at Canton. Sun Yat-sen appoints Chiang Kai-shek the organiser of the new army. Wu P'ei-fu, the warlord favoured by the British, is driven from Peking and power given to Feng Yu'-hsiang. Chang Tso-lin allies with Feng
1925 **March:** Sun dies, Feng is ousted from Peking, and Chang rules. The British use gunfire to disperse demonstrations at Shanghai **(30th May)** and Canton **(23rd June)**
1926 Chiang Kai-shek's northern campaign against the warlords
1927 **18th April:** Chiang and the conservative members of the Kuomintang set up a new government at Nanking
1927 The landless are organised on the Communist model in Kiangsi
-34 and adjacent Fukien and under Mao Tse-tung and Chu Teh they defend themselves against attacks from the Nanking government
1934 The Communists are dislodged and set out on the Long March
1937 The Shensi government is brought into harmony with Nanking Japan harasses China in a series of territorial conquests
1940 **20th March:** a puppet Chinese government headed by Wang Ching-wei is established at Nanking with the support of the Japanese
1943 **13th September:** Chiang Kai-shek is elected president of the Chinese Republic
1944 **26th August-11th October:** negotiations between Chiang and Mao fail to resolve their differences and heavy fighting results
1949 **21st January:** Chiang resigns the presidency leaving Vice-President Li Tsung-jen in charge of peace talks with the Communists
1st October: the Communist People's Republic of China is officially proclaimed at Peking with Mao Tse-tung as chairman of the people's administrative council and Chou En-lai as premier and foreign minister
8th December: the United Nations recognises China's independence

Top: American police station in Peking at the time of the Boxer Rising (left); Yüan Shih-k'ai, the man who betrayed the early Republic (middle); the face of old China (right). **Centre:** *Shanghai —in the thirties (left) and in 1940, with British troops, led by an American marines band, departing for the last time (right).* **Bottom:** *A 1931 Soviet poster cheers on the Chinese Communists (left); Mao Tse-tung during the People's War of Liberation (middle); a peasant roundly denounces his landlord (right)*

Index of main people, places, and events

Author's suggestions for further reading

General histories:
McAleavy, Henry
The Modern History of China
Weidenfeld and Nicolson 1967
Clubb, O.Edmund
Twentieth-Century China
Columbia University Press 1964
FitzGerald, CP
The Birth of Communist China
Penguin Books 1964
Reischauer, E O and
Fairbank, J K
*East Asia: The Modern Trans-
formation*
Allen and Unwin 1961

Books on particular topics:
Fleming, Peter
The Siege at Peking
Hart-Davis 1959
Chen, Jerome
Yüan Shih-k'ai
Allen and Unwin 1961
Isaacs, Harold
*The Tragedy of the Chinese
Revolution*
Oxford University Press 1961
North, Robert C
*Moscow and the Chinese
Communists*
Oxford University Press 1963
Schwartz, Benjamin I
*Chinese Communism and the
Rise of Mao*
Oxford University Press 1963
Schwartz, Benjamin I
Mao and the Chinese Revolution
Oxford University Press 1968
Chassin, L M
*The Communist Conquest of
China*
Weidenfeld and Nicolson 1966
Schram, Stuart R
Mao Tse-tung
Penguin Books 1966
Donnithorne, Audrey
China's Economic System
Allen and Unwin 1967
Gray, Jack and
Cavendish, Patrick
Chinese Communism in Crisis
Pall Mall 1968

Library of the 20th Century will include the following titles:

Russia in Revolt
David Floyd
The Second Reich
Harold Kurtz
The Anarchists
Roderick Kedward
Suffragettes International
Trevor Lloyd
War by Time-Table
A J P Taylor
Death of a Generation
Alistair Horne
Suicide of the Empires
Alan Clark
Twilight of the Habsburgs
Z A B Zeman
Early Aviation
Sir Robert Saundby
Birth of the Movies
D J Wenden
America Comes of Age
A E Campbell
Lenin's Russia
G Katkov
The Weimar Republic
Sefton Delmer
Out of the Lion's Paw
Constantine Fitzgibbon
Japan: The Years of Triumph
Louis Allen
Communism Takes China
CPFitzGerald
Black and White in South Africa
G H Le May
Woodrow Wilson
R H Ferrell
France 1918-34
W Knapp
France 1934-40
A N Wahl
Mussolini's Italy
Geoffrey Warner
The Little Dictators
A Polonsky
Viva Zapata
L Bethell
The World Depression
Malcolm Falkus
Stalin's Russia
A Nove
The Brutal Reich
Donald Watt
The Spanish Civil War
Raymond Carr
Munich: Czech Tragedy
K G Robbins

CPFitzGerald was born in London in 1902. He is currently Professor of Far Eastern History at the Australian National University, Canberra. Between 1923 and 1939 he lived in China and returned there after the war. From 1946 to 1950 he was a representative of the British Council in North China. His works include *China: A Short Cultural History, The Empress Wu, The Third China, The Birth of Communist China,* and *A Concise History of East Asia*

JM Roberts, General Editor of the *Macdonald Library of the 20th Century,* is Fellow and Tutor in Modern History at Merton College, Oxford. He was also General Editor of Purnell's *History of the 20th Century,* is Joint-Editor of the *English Historical Review,* and author of *Europe 1880-1945* in the Longmans History of Europe. He has been English Editor of the *Larousse Encyclopedia of Modern History,* has reviewed for *The Observer, New Statesman,* and *Spectator,* and given talks on the BBC.

Library of the 20th Century

Editor: Jonathan Martin
Executive Editor: Richard Johnson
Editorial Assistant: Jenny Ashby
Designed by: Brian Mayers/ Germano Facetti
Research: Evan Davies

Pictures selected from the following sources

Associated Press 97 107 123
Auckland Collection 9
Barnaby's 122 123
Black Star 101 105 108 113
British Museum 14
D Bryan 4
Camera Press 10 13 105 115 121
Central Press 8 89 109
Documentation Chinoise Paris 41
Editions Rencontre 78 83
John Hillelson Agency 22 27 67 87 123
Hsinhua News Agency 60
Keystone 8 50 85 91 97 103 119
Kladder Adatsch 69 80
J Klugman Collection 111
Kunstgewerbe Museum Zurich 122
Library of Congress 122
Magnum Rene Burri 81
Magnum H Cartier Bresson 128
Marc Riboud 123
Novosti 47 54
Pictorial Press 117
Radio Times Hulton 18 20 26 29 39 43 56 65
N Ringart Paris 37
W Sewell 11
G Sirot 123
Snark International 35 58 80
Society for Anglo-Chinese Understanding 75
Südd Verlag 56 95
Syndication International 33
United Press International 7
USIS 88
Victoria and Albert Museum 16
Roger Viollet 31 45 49 53 63 93

If we have unwittingly infringed copyright in any picture or photograph reproduced in this publication, we tender our sincere apologies and will be glad of the opportunity, upon being satisfied as to the owner's title, to pay an appropriate fee as if we had been able to obtain prior permission